Following a long career in advertising, Kim Terakes now devotes himself exclusively to the cause of good food. Over the last two decades, Kim has written extensively about food and restaurants for publications such as *Australian Gourmet Traveller*, *Vogue Entertaining*, *BRW*, *SMH Good Living*, *GQ*, the *Sunday Telegraph* and the *SMH Good Food Guide*. Kim also runs the Boys Can Cook cooking school and Australia's largest barbecue club, aussiebarbie.com.au. He is Australia's go-to barbecue expert, appearing regularly on *A Current Affair*, *The Circle*, *Kerri-Anne Kennerley* and *Sydney Weekender* and doing regular guest spots on 702 ABC and 2UE radio. His previous books, *The Great Aussie Barbie Cookbook*, *The Great Aussie Bloke's Cookbook*, *The Great Aussie Family Cookbook* and *The Great Aussie Asian Cookbook* are also published by Penguin. Kim's website is kimterakes.com.

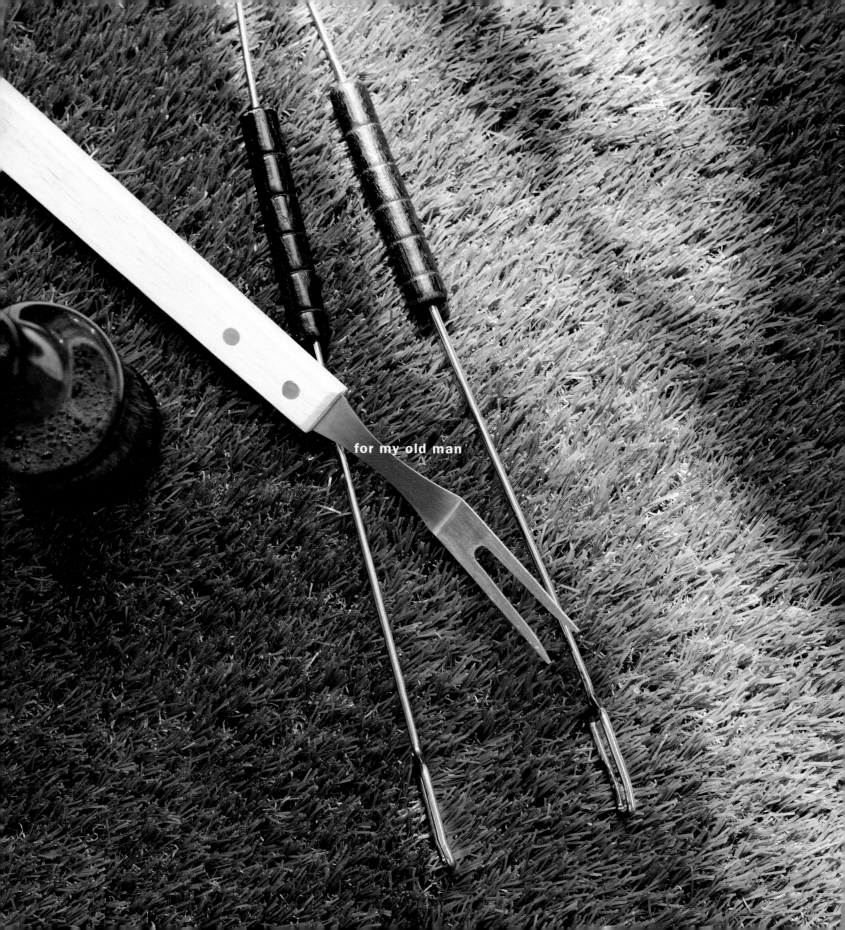

for my old man

THE GREAT
Aussie
Barbie
COOKBOOK
FAST & EASY

Kim Terakes

Photography by Rob Palmer

VIKING
an imprint of
PENGUIN BOOKS

INTRODUCTION 3

BREKKIE & BRUNCH 5

BEEF 69

LAMB 91

SALAD & VEG 163

DESSERT 183

COLD
STARTERS 29

HOT
STARTERS
49

CHICKEN

135 SEAFOOD

&PORK'''

INDEX 200

THANKS
199

KIMBO'S TEN BARBECUE COMMANDMENTS

1 Thou shalt clean the hotplate.
Blokes just don't get hygiene. Just because the hotplate gets very hot, it doesn't mean that the layer of grease, insects and worse from your last barbie will disappear.

Note: pouring beer on it doesn't mean the beer fairies make it disappear, either.

2 Thou shalt eat wonderful food.
What does the term 'barbecue steak' mean? Does it mean meat that's a bit ordinary, but good enough for a barbecue? Just because it's 'only a barbie', that is not an excuse to eat third-rate produce – buy the best you can afford and enjoy its quality. You can, of course, use top-quality cheaper cuts of meat, chicken thighs instead of breasts and splendidly oily fish, perfect for the barbecue.

3 Thou shalt not burn the bum out of things.
If you are going to use your barbecue as an oven by closing the lid, you can't have any heat directly under the baking dish or you will burn the bum out of whatever you're cooking. The idea is to have the heat surrounding the dish.

4 Thou shalt not cook cold meat.
Always bring the meat or poultry back to room temperature so it cooks evenly. The bigger the piece, the longer it will need to come to room temperature. You don't of course want to stick anything in the sun in the middle of the day; just find a cool place in the kitchen.

5 Thou shalt not feed fat to the chargrill.
Cooking fatty meats like chops on the chargrill seems like a good idea, because the fat runs out, but it catches fire and burns the meat. Cook your chops on the hotplate first and finish them on the chargrill.

6 Thou shalt not torture the steaks.
Turn the bloody steak once, not twice and certainly not 20 times if you want a nice caramelised crust on it.

7 Thou shalt not poke the sausages.
Spearing the sausages not only dries them out, but lets the fat drip onto the naked flame so they incinerate and turn to charcoal.

8 Thou shalt not poison the guests.
Further to blokes and hygiene. Don't put cooked meat back on the plate that it came to the barbecue on raw, and don't put uncooked leftover marinade on cooked meat.

9 Thou shalt rest after barbecuing.
You can rest later, but the steak or chook needs to rest a few minutes somewhere warm, loosely covered with foil or a clean tea towel, to allow the juices to relax back into the fibres of the meat. Again, the bigger the piece of meat, the longer it will need, so allow longer for roasts.

10 Thou shalt enjoy thyself.
What else could you do at an Aussie barbie?

INTRODUCTION

Don't get me wrong – I LOVE slow-cooked food.

BUT we don't always have half a day or more to devote to dinner, especially around the barbecue, when a meal is just part of a life that includes ferrying kids to soccer, ballet or netball, not to mention birthday parties (how many friends can one kid have?), as well as a bit of time for yourself to go to the footy, the hairdresser, the hardware store, the movies, or for a drink with some chums.

Which is why I have written *The Great Aussie Barbie Fast and Easy Cookbook*.

It's my fifth tome in as many years and it seems to be what people want these days: quick, easy food that is both delicious and a bit more interesting than just steaks and bangers on the barbie. What's more, for these recipes you don't have to scour the shelves of specialist shops for esoteric ingredients. I'm not saying that everything will be at the two major supermarkets, but 90 per cent will.

Having said that, I do encourage you to buy your meat from a quality butcher and your seafood from the markets or the best local fishmonger that you can find. Talk to your meat, seafood and fruit merchants about what's fresh, and what they think is the best product in their shop. Barbecuing, like cooking of any kind, is so simply all about the quality of the ingredients.

You should be able to cook virtually everything in here in about half an hour, without being silly and putting a stopwatch on the process. The exceptions are the recipes that call for marinating, which is dead easy and just allows you to insert a soccer/ballet/ hairdresser/movie option in between.

We covered a lot of the basics in my first book, *The Great Aussie Barbie Cookbook*, so we won't repeat all that here. Most of my tips come down to common sense or just giving things a bit of thought.

Make a shopping list.
I make a list with columns for fruit and veg, the butcher, seafood, supermarket, specialty things, booze and pantry items. It's hardly the highlight of my week but it sure beats multiple trips back to the shops.

Soak your sticks.
Because little sticks of wood are pretty good at burning and we use little sticks of wood to skewer food on the barbie, you need to soak the wooden skewers in water for a couple of hours before you use them. If you prefer, you could use metal skewers.

Keep a spare gas bottle.
It is a real pain in the neck to run out of gas with a house full of people and a barbecue covered in half-cooked steaks. As you are driving to the service station to get a replacement, a spare gas bottle seems like a pretty good idea.

Think about the time.
Work out how long the meat will take to cook and how long it will need to rest and then figure out when you need to, say, grill the vegetables so they'll all be ready at the same time. Also, it is worth thinking about all the non-food things that you will need on the day, like plates, platters, glasses and so on and have them all out so you're not running around while your steak is getting cold.

Use the right oil.
Olive oil, especially expensive extra virgin olive oil, is great for salad dressings but wasted splashed on a barbecue. Use ordinary olive oil on hotplates, and what I call neutral oil – in that it doesn't impart any flavour of its own – for shallow-frying and stir-frying. Good examples of neutral oils are peanut oil, vegetable oil, safflower oil and canola. Buy young olive oils – old is generally bad and 'Lite' olive oil is nonsense.

Finally, if all else fails, follow Kimbo's Ten Barbecue Commandments, on the opposite page.

Huevos rancheros (Mexican fried eggs)

PREP **10 mins**   COOK **17 mins**

Now these will either cure you or kill you, chillies for brekkie not being a regular practice for most of us. Nothing here takes long or is very complicated, but you do need to be able to do a few things at once.

There are lots of options ingredients-wise, with the eggs and the tortillas being the only compulsory items.

You can include a simple salsa, which I will. I have used re-fried beans or black beans and you could also add feta, cheddar or sour cream and, of course, more chillies.

1 cup (300 g) canned black beans, rinsed and drained, or 1 cup (240 g) re-fried beans
4 small corn tortillas
8 free-range or organic eggs
extra olive oil for frying
1 cup (120 g) grated cheddar cheese
2 tablespoons coriander leaves, roughly chopped

SALSA
2 tablespoons olive oil
1 red onion, finely sliced
2 cloves garlic, finely sliced
1 jalapeno chilli, seeded and finely sliced
2 large tomatoes, seeded and finely diced
½ teaspoon Tabasco (optional)

1 To make the salsa, heat the olive oil in a small pan, then add the onion, garlic and chilli and cook for 5 minutes over low–medium heat until soft. Add the tomatoes and Tabasco, if using, and cook for another 5 minutes.
2 Warm the beans in another saucepan for about 5 minutes (or cheat and warm them in the microwave) and gently warm the tortillas on a preheated chargrill.
3 Fry the eggs in the olive oil on a preheated flat grillplate over high heat for about 2 minutes until cooked sunny side up. Place each tortilla on a separate plate, with two eggs on top. Divide the beans and salsa evenly between the tortillas and top with grated cheese and coriander leaves.

Serves 4

BREKKIE & BRUNCH

Apple and cinnamon hotcakes

PREP **10 mins**   COOK **15 mins**

Just because it's brekkie doesn't mean you can't break out the barbie.

Simple little hotcakes like this are easy as long as you've cleaned the hotplate recently. Don't even think about them if you haven't.

If you want to make these for dessert instead, serve with ice-cream instead of yoghurt.

40 g butter
2 granny smith apples, peeled, cored and
  chopped into ½ cm dice
1 teaspoon ground cinnamon
3 tablespoons caster sugar
4 free-range or organic eggs, separated
1 teaspoon vanilla extract
300 ml buttermilk
2 cups (300 g) self-raising flour
pinch of salt
neutral oil, for frying
yoghurt, to serve
maple syrup, to serve

1 Heat the butter in a frying pan over low–medium heat, then add the apple and cook for 3–4 minutes until soft. Add the cinnamon and one tablespoon of the caster sugar and cook, stirring for about 1 minute until the sugar dissolves. Transfer the apples and any cooking juices to a bowl to cool.

2 In a large mixing bowl, beat the egg yolks with the remaining caster sugar and vanilla extract until the yolks turn pale yellow. Whisk through the buttermilk, then fold through the flour and a pinch of salt.

3 In a clean bowl, beat the eggwhites until stiff and fold them through the egg yolk mixture, then gently fold through the cooked apple and any juices.

4 Heat a little oil on a preheated flat grillplate, then, working in batches, spoon about 2 tablespoons of the mixture onto the grill. Cook the hotcakes on one side for 1–2 minutes until bubbles appear on the surface, then cook on the other side for 1–2 minutes. When cooked, remove from the grill and keep them warm while you cook the rest. Serve topped with yoghurt and maple syrup.

Serves 4 – makes about 12 hotcakes

BREKKIE & BRUNCH

Mushroom and haloumi bruschetta

PREP **10 mins**   COOK **6–8 mins**

Here's a recipe that works as a light brunch on its own or before a serious piece of meat on a chilly winter's day. You need to serve the haloumi pretty quickly after cooking. Just cooked, it is salty and delicious, with a lovely soft texture, but it will dry out and go hard in 15 minutes.

8 field mushrooms, wiped clean
neutral oil, for cooking
4 thick slices rustic Italian bread, such as ciabatta
1 packet (250 g) haloumi cheese, cut into ½ cm slices
1 clove garlic, halved
handful of baby rocket leaves

DRESSING
120 ml olive oil
3 tablespoons balsamic vinegar
½ red chilli, seeded and finely sliced
12 mint leaves, finely sliced
sea salt and freshly ground black pepper, to taste

1 To make the dressing, mix all ingredients together in a small bowl, then set dressing aside while you do the cooking.
2 Brush the mushrooms with a little oil and cook them on a preheated flat grillplate over medium heat for about 1 minute on each side. Set aside.
3 Brush the bread with a little oil, then grill it on a preheated chargrill over high heat for about 1 minute on each side. At the same time, grill the haloumi slices for about 1–2 minutes on each side.
4 Rub one side of each slice of bread well with the cut garlic. Place on four plates, garlic side up, and top with some rocket leaves. Place two mushrooms on each piece, and the haloumi slices on top.
5 Spoon a little of the dressing over the top of each bruschetta and serve immediately.

Serves 4

Bruschetta with figs, goat's cheese, basil and honey >

PREP **5 mins**   COOK **3 mins**

Some flavours seem to work magically together and these are right up there. You could add some thinly sliced prosciutto if you wanted to de-vego the dish.

If you see that figs are in season (they are usually great late March–early April), grab a couple and whip this up for a five-minute brunch the next day.

4 thick slices rustic Italian bread, such as ciabatta
3 tablespoons olive oil
250 g fresh goat's cheese, crumbled
6 fresh figs, quartered
2 teaspoons honey
8 basil leaves, torn
freshly ground black pepper, to taste

1 Grill the bread on a preheated chargrill over high heat until browned on both sides, then place on plates.
2 Drizzle two tablespoons of the olive oil over the bruschetta, then divide the goat's cheese and fig quarters evenly between them. Drizzle the remaining oil and the honey over the top, then sprinkle with basil leaves and season with pepper.

Serves 4

< Baked Italian sausages with fennel and tomato

PREP **10 mins**   COOK **35 mins**

You're probably not going to knock this off before your morning gym session and 15-kilometre jog. It's more a lazy autumn brunch that rolls into lunch and a glass of wine sort of dish. Kids love it too.

½ cup (125 ml) olive oil
1 large brown onion, cut into ½ cm slices
1 small bulb fennel, core removed, cut into ½ cm slices
2 cloves garlic, finely sliced
2 × 400 g cans diced tomatoes
½ cup (125 ml) white wine
8 Italian-style pork or pork and fennel sausages
2 tablespoons balsamic vinegar
2 tablespoons flat-leaf parsley leaves, roughly chopped
polenta or mashed potato, to serve

1 In a flameproof baking dish large enough to hold the sausages comfortably, heat the olive oil over medium heat then add the onion, fennel and garlic and cook for 6–10 minutes or until lightly browned.
2 Add the tomatoes and wine, bring to the boil and simmer for 5 minutes, then add the sausages, pushing them down so that they are covered with the liquid.
3 Place baking dish in the middle of the barbecue, with heat surrounding it on both sides, but not directly underneath. Close the hood and cook for 15–20 minutes, until the sausages are brown and cooked through.
4 To serve, place a couple of sausages with sauce on each serving plate and top with a drizzle of balsamic vinegar and the parsley leaves. Serve with polenta or mashed potato.

Serves 4

Corn fritters with smoked salmon

PREP **10 mins**   COOK **20–25 mins**

A generation ago you would never have considered this for breakfast, and now it is absolutely standard breakfast or brunch fare in cafés around the country. I would always use corn cooked on the cob, but feel free to use frozen corn kernels instead.

butter, for frying
8 slices smoked salmon or ocean trout
2 cups (500 g) mascarpone
1 tablespoon chives, finely chopped
freshly ground black pepper, to taste
lime wedges

CORN FRITTERS
1½ corn cobs, or 1½ cups (240 g) frozen corn kernels
25 g butter
3 free-range or organic eggs, separated
1 cup (250 ml) milk
120 g plain flour
1 heaped teaspoon baking powder
½ teaspoon salt

1 To make the fritters, bring a large saucepan of water to the boil, add the corn and cook, covered, for 10–15 minutes or until the corn is tender. Gently remove the corn from the pot and transfer to a plate. Once cool enough to handle, stand each corn cob up on a chopping board and carefully slice the kernels off with a large knife. Set aside the kernels.
2 Melt the butter in a small pan over medium heat. In a large mixing bowl, beat the egg yolks then gradually add the milk. In a separate bowl, beat the eggwhites until they are stiff. Sift the flour and baking powder into the egg yolk mixture, fold through the eggwhites and then the melted butter and salt. Fold in the corn kernels and refrigerate the batter, covered, until ready to cook.
3 Heat a little butter on a preheated flat grillplate over medium–hot heat. Carefully ladle a couple of tablespoons of the batter at a time onto the hot grill, and cook for about 2 minutes on each side.
4 Put two fritters on each plate, then place a slice of smoked salmon on top of each fritter. Top with a dollop of mascarpone and some chives.
5 Season with pepper, and garnish with a lime quarter.

Serves 4, makes 8–12 fritters

BREKKIE & BRUNCH

13

Grilled chicken Caesar salad

PREP **10 mins**   COOK **10–15 mins**   REST **5 mins**

I used to love watching grand old black-tied waiters making Caesar Salad from scratch in grand old silver service restaurants. You can impress the pants off your chums by basically doing the same thing in a bowl beside the barbecue, sans black tie.

Being a purist, I have always objected to anything superfluous being included in a proper Caesar, but given that the grilled chicken version has become such a café standard these days, who am I to buck the system? You could always cheat and use good-quality store-bought mayonnaise and add the anchovies.

**12 slices thin sourdough bread or baguette
  (or cheat and use a packet of croutons)**
1 rasher thick, rindless bacon, cut into 1 cm pieces
2 free-range or organic eggs
olive oil for rubbing
2–3 chicken tenderloins or 1 breast fillet
**1 baby cos or ½ cos lettuce, washed, drained and
  cut into 6–8 cm pieces**
25 g parmesan cheese, shaved
sea salt and freshly ground black pepper, to taste

MAYONNAISE
4 anchovy fillets
1 free-range or organic egg yolk
1 teaspoon Dijon mustard
½ cup (125 ml) olive oil
2 tablespoons lemon juice

1 To make the croutons, cut the crusts off the sourdough or baguette slices and toast them on a preheated chargrill over medium heat until browned on both sides. Set aside to cool.

2 Fry the bacon on a preheated flat grillplate over medium heat for about 3–4 minutes until it is brown and slightly crispy, then drain it on a paper towel.

3 Put the eggs in cold water in a small saucepan, bring to the boil, then simmer for 5 minutes. Rinse immediately under cold water. Once the eggs have cooled, peel and quarter them.

4 To cook the chicken, rub it with a little olive oil and season well with salt and pepper, then cook on a preheated chargrill for a few minutes on each side. Remove from the grill and set aside to rest, loosely covered with foil, for 5 minutes while you make the dressing.

5 Take a bowl large enough to hold the finished salad and let the theatre begin.

6 First, to make the mayonnaise, place the anchovies in the bowl and break them up with a fork. Mix in the egg yolk and mustard. Add the oil drop by drop at first until the dressing thickens, and then in a thin stream until it has a thick, eggy consistency, beating all the time with the fork or a small whisk. When thick, beat through the lemon juice. Gently toss the cos lettuce through the mayo, then add the bacon and croutons. Divide salad evenly between plates.

7 Slice the chicken and arrange it, with the quartered eggs, on top of the salad. Scatter the parmesan on top and finish by seasoning with salt and pepper.

Serves 4

Steak sandwich with beetroot relish

PREP 10 mins   COOK 30 mins   REST 5 mins

Nothing can beat a footy club steak sambo for me – white bread, rough-and-ready onions and probably No Frills salt and tomato sauce. But for entertaining, let's head in the opposite direction with something a bit more upmarket that still tastes great.

4 × 1–1½ cm slices beef scotch fillet
1 tablespoon olive oil
sea salt and freshly ground black pepper, to taste
4 pieces focaccia or Turkish bread about the same size as the steaks, cut in half horizontally
⅓ cup (80 ml) plain yoghurt
handful of baby rocket leaves

BEETROOT RELISH
1 tablespoon butter
1 spring onion, white and pale-green parts only, finely sliced
2 beetroot, peeled and cut into fine matchsticks
4 sprigs dill, leaves only
½ teaspoon finely grated orange zest
2 tablespoons fresh orange juice
½ cup (125 ml) beef or veal stock
sea salt and freshly ground black pepper, to taste

1 To make the relish, melt the butter in a saucepan over medium heat and add the spring onion, stirring until it softens slightly. Add the beetroot, stirring to coat with butter, then add the other ingredients and bring to the boil (this should take about 3–5 minutes) before reducing heat to a simmer. Allow to cook down to a jammy consistency, about 20–25 minutes.
2 As the relish is approaching the right consistency, brush the steaks with oil and season with a little salt and pepper, then cook on a preheated chargrill over high heat for about 3–4 minutes on each side. Rest, loosely covered with foil, for 5 minutes before serving.
3 Lightly brush the bread with oil, then cook on a preheated chargrill for about 1–2 minutes.
4 Remove bread from barbecue and spread it with the yoghurt. Top with rocket leaves, steak, some more salt and a big dollop of the relish before adding the other slice of bread.

Serves 4

Bloody Mary prawn cocktail >

PREP 15 mins

Do the decent thing and wait until the sun is well and truly over the 10 a.m. mark before you tackle these – then try these crustacean treats with a Bloody Mary to wash them down. Seriously, there's a lovely spicy, salty thing going on here that is perfect for a late Sunday brekkie with mates that drifts into a lunchtime barbie.

24 cooked king prawns
1 stalk celery, finely sliced
2 cups cos or iceberg lettuce, shredded
freshly ground black pepper, to taste
8 quail eggs (optional), hard-boiled and peeled
1 tablespoon celery salt (optional)

COCKTAIL SAUCE
1 cup (250 ml) tomato sauce
1 tablespoon Worcestershire sauce
1 teaspoon Tabasco sauce
1 tablespoon vodka

1 To make the sauce, mix all ingredients together in a small jug and place in the refrigerator.
2 To prepare the prawns, twist off the head and carefully remove the shell. With a sharp knife, make a 5 mm-deep cut down the back, then remove the dark intestinal vein, leaving the last section of tail on if you like. Set aside somewhere cool.
3 Combine celery and lettuce and place in four cocktail glasses or small dishes. Arrange six prawns on top of each, and drizzle sauce over the top, serving remaining sauce on the side. Season with pepper just before serving. If you like, serve with quail eggs dipped in celery salt.

Serves 4

BREKKIE & BRUNCH

Carne asada tortilla (Barbecued steak tortilla)

PREP 15 mins   MARINATE 4 hrs   COOK 4–6 mins   REST 5–10 mins

This is a classic Mexican recipe which feeds lots of people for lunch very easily. Just put out a bowl of tomato salsa, some avocado slices or guacamole, warmed tortillas and a plate of the spicy, sliced steaks and let your guests go for their lives.

1 kg topside, skirt or flank steak, cut into 1 cm slices
2 tablespoons olive oil
1 large avocado, cut into thin slices, or 1 generous cup of guacamole (see page 42)
8 flour or corn tortillas

MARINADE
1 teaspoon cumin seeds
3 cloves garlic, crushed
1 jalapeno chilli, seeded and finely sliced
½ cup coriander leaves and stalks, roughly chopped
1 tablespoon white-wine vinegar
1 teaspoon Tabasco
½ cup (125 ml) lime juice
¼ cup (60 ml) orange juice
sea salt and freshly ground black pepper, to taste

PICO DE GALLO (TOMATO SALSA)
2 tomatoes, seeded and chopped into 1 cm dice
½ red onion, finely diced
½–1 jalapeno chilli, seeded and finely sliced
handful of coriander leaves, finely chopped
½ teaspoon ground cumin
2 tablespoons lime juice

1 To make the marinade, place the cumin seeds in a mortar and pestle and grind them to break them up (but not to a powder). Add garlic, chilli and coriander and grind to a coarse paste. Combine paste with the rest of the marinade ingredients in a shallow glass or ceramic bowl, and add the steak, turning to coat thoroughly. Cover with plastic film and leave in the fridge to marinate for 4 hours.

2 To make the tomato salsa, mix all the ingredients together in a serving bowl and place in the fridge.

3 Bring the meat to room temperature by removing from the fridge half an hour before cooking. Remove steak from the marinade, then cook the steak in the oil on a preheated flat grillplate or chargrill over high heat for 4–6 minutes. Rest it for 5–10 minutes in a shallow bowl, then slice it thinly across the grain into ½ cm slices, and return it to the resting bowl with any juices.

4 Warm the tortillas for a few seconds on the flat grillplate, then remove them. To serve, carefully place meat slices, avocado slices and salsa on each tortilla and roll them up. Wash them down with a Corona.

Serves 4

< Baked beans with bacon

PREP 10 mins   COOK 15 mins

Here you can fry the bacon on the flat grillplate of your barbecue while you cook the beans and sauce on the wok burner. The whole exercise shouldn't take more than 20 minutes or so and this is such a delicious way to start the day – even if it doesn't make you lovely to be around.

1 rasher thick, rindless bacon, cut into pieces 3 cm × 1 cm
2 tablespoons olive oil
1 onion, grated, or very finely chopped
1 clove garlic, crushed
1 teaspoon mustard powder
1 teaspoon sweet paprika
½ teaspoon cayenne pepper (optional)
1 tablespoon tomato paste
1 × 400 g can diced tomatoes
1 tablespoon pure maple syrup
1 × 400 g can borlotti beans, drained and rinsed
1 × 400 g can cannellini beans, drained and rinsed
1 small handful of flat-leaf parsley leaves, roughly chopped
toasted sourdough bread or muffins, to serve

1 Fry the bacon on a preheated flat grillplate over medium heat for about 3–4 minutes until it is brown and slightly crispy, then drain it on a paper towel and set aside.
2 Heat the olive oil in a wok or large saucepan and cook the onion and garlic until soft. Stir in the mustard and paprika plus the cayenne, if using, then immediately add the tomato paste, diced tomatoes and maple syrup. Stir to incorporate the ingredients and simmer for 5 minutes on low heat.
3 Add the beans and the reserved bacon and simmer for another 5 minutes on low heat until the beans are heated through. Gently fold through the chopped parsley leaves.
4 Serve with toasted sourdough bread or muffins.

Serves 4

Grilled mortadella, red capsicum and eggplant sambo

PREP 10 mins   COOK 20 mins

For some reason, grilling thin slices of mortadella has become ever so trendy in smart little Italian restaurants. So why miss out at home?

Set your flat grillplate on medium heat for the eggplant and capsicum and your chargrill on high for the mortadella.

It's up to you whether you eat these as plain sambos, or throw them on the flat grillplate to toast them and melt the bocconcini.

⅓ cup (80 ml) olive oil
2 red capsicums, white insides and seeds removed, cut into 2 cm strips
1 eggplant, cut into ½ cm slices
12–16 slices mortadella
250 g bocconcini, thinly sliced
4 individual foccacia rolls, or enough foccacia or Italian bread such as ciabatta to make 4 generous sambos
1 teaspoon dried oregano leaves
handful of baby rocket
freshly ground black pepper, to taste

1 Pour 1 tablespoon of oil onto a preheated flat grillplate and cook capsicum over medium heat for about 10 minutes, until it softens, turning frequently. Remove from grill and keep warm. Cook eggplant slices in the rest of the oil on the flat grillplate over medium heat for about 5 minutes. Remove from grill and keep warm.
2 Cook the mortadella on a preheated chargrill over high heat for about 1 minute until the slices scorch a little and caramelise. Remove and reserve.
3 Place the sliced cheese on the bottom piece of bread and sprinkle with oregano. Place the mortadella slices on top, then add the capsicum, eggplant and rocket leaves. Season with plenty of pepper and cover with a piece of bread to make a sandwich.
4 Eat as they are, or cook on flat grillplate or chargrill over medium heat for 2–3 minutes on each side, until warmed through and slightly crisp, turning carefully once.

Serves 4

Zucchini fritters with ras el hanout prawns

PREP **20 mins**   COOK **10–15 mins**

Let's say these are more brunch than breakfast, and maybe a late-ish brunch at that. Maybe even with a Bloody Mary to get the heart started. I love the prawns on their own, as finger food – again, with a Bloody Mary. In case you're wondering, ras el hanout is a Moroccan spice blend, made with up to 30 spices, available from specialty food stores.

8–12 green (raw) king prawns
2 teaspoons cumin seeds
1 red onion, very finely sliced then roughly chopped
1 clove garlic, crushed
⅓ cup (80 ml) olive oil
3 zucchini, coarsely grated
1 teaspoon ground coriander
2 free-range or organic eggs, separated
1 tablespoon parsley, finely chopped
½ teaspoon finely grated lemon zest
½ cup (75 g) self-raising flour
sea salt and freshly ground black pepper, to taste
2 tablespoons ras el hanout
rocket, to serve (optional)
lime halves, to serve (optional)

1 To prepare the prawns, twist off the head and carefully remove the shell. With a sharp knife, make a 5 mm-deep cut down the back, then remove the dark intestinal vein, leaving the last section of tail on if you like. Set aside somewhere cool.

2 Cook cumin seeds in a dry pan over medium heat for 1–2 minutes until they are fragrant and slightly darker. Set aside.

3 Fry the onion and garlic in a tablespoon of the oil in a non-stick frying pan over medium heat until soft. Allow to cool a little, and then, in a large mixing bowl, mix together with the zucchini, cumin, coriander, egg yolks, parsley, lemon zest and flour. Season well with salt and pepper.

4 In a clean bowl, beat the eggwhites until stiff and fold through the vegetable mixture.

5 Toss prawns in a tablespoon of oil then sprinkle ras el hanout and salt generously on both sides.

6 Spread the remaining oil over preheated flat grillplate on medium heat, and ladle out enough mixture to make 10–12 cm fritters (about 2–3 tablespoons each). Turn the fritters after about 2 minutes, when the bottom is golden-brown and bubbles appear on the surface.

7 While you are making the fritters, cook the prawns on the flat grillplate or chargrill for about 2–3 minutes on each side.

8 Transfer the fritters to serving plates and top with the prawns. Serve with a little dressed rocket and lime halves if you like.

Serves 4

Quesadillas

PREP 5–10 mins   COOK 5 mins

These things are harder to pronounce than to cook. Think Kay-sar-dee-yars and forget any 'qu' or 'dill' sounds. They're as simple as this: get some large tortillas from the supermarket, put some good flavours and cheese on one half, fold them over and throw them on to a preheated chargrill and cook until they have nice chargrilled marks on them, or until the cheese has melted and they're warmed through.

No recipes here, just some different ideas for fillings.

Try:

- leftover chilli and cheddar
- ham and gruyere
- diced tomato, corn kernels (canned or frozen), sliced jalapeno, coriander and a little cream cheese
- 1 × 400 g can of cannellini beans, tomato, oregano and provolone, or
- mortadella, finely chopped sun-dried tomatoes and grated parmesan.

Crispy misters (Croque monsieurs)

PREP 5 mins   COOK 4–6 mins

Croque Monsieurs are the famous Parisian snacks that date back over one hundred years. Translating roughly to crispy misters, which sounds much sillier, they're nothing more than a buttery ham and cheese toasted sandwich with mustard. Then again, they don't need to be any more than that.

100 g butter, softened
8 slices thick white bread
2 tablespoons Dijon mustard
8–12 thin slices leg ham
2 cups (250 g) grated gruyere cheese
sea salt and freshly ground black pepper, to taste

1 Butter the bread slices on both sides. Spread the mustard over four slices of bread and pile 2–3 ham slices on top of each, then divide the cheese between them. Season with salt and pepper and place a slice of bread on top of each.
2 Cook on a preheated flat grillplate over medium heat for about 2–3 minutes each side, until the sandwiches are golden-brown and the cheese has melted.

Serves 4

< Zucchini frittata

PREP 10 mins   COOK 15–20 mins

Frittatas have provided some relief from a thousand hangovers when I've found leftovers in the fridge. I always make them too big deliberately. Frittatas are like risottos; once you understand the basic technique, there are dozens of different flavours that you can use. The trick with both is to keep them nice and simple.

1 onion, very finely sliced
1 clove garlic, crushed
2 zucchini, grated
1 tablespoon olive oil
8 free-range or organic eggs
1 small handful of flat-leaf parsley leaves, roughly chopped
1 small handful of mint leaves, roughly chopped
½ cup (40 g) grated parmesan
1 teaspoon butter
green salad, to serve (optional)

1 Fry the onion, garlic and zucchini in the oil in a non-stick frying pan over medium heat until soft. Transfer to a bowl and allow to cool slightly. Wipe the pan clean.
2 Break the eggs into a large mixing bowl and beat with a fork, adding parsley, mint and cheese, and then fold the vegetables through.
3 Melt the butter in a non-stick frying pan over very low heat on your wok burner, pour in the egg mixture and spread evenly. Put the lid on or cover tightly with foil and cook for about 15 minutes. The trick is to cook the frittata through to the top without burning the bottom.
4 Slide the frittata out of the frying pan and slice. Serve cold or at room temperature, either on its own or with a little green salad.

Serves 4 as a light meal and 6–8 as a snack

Piperade with scrambled eggs and chorizo

PREP 15 mins   COOK 25 mins

Piperade, made of braised tomato and capsicum, is a real fave in the Terakes household, and has been seen on the dinner table just as often as the brekkie or brunch table.

Great big salty and sweet flavours and nicely contrasting textures. It all works gangbusters.

⅓ cup (80 ml) olive oil
1 or 2 chorizo sausages, finely sliced
1 onion, finely chopped
2 cloves garlic, finely chopped
1 red capsicum, white pith and seeds removed, cut into 1–2 cm pieces
1 green capsicum, white pith and seeds removed, cut into 1–2 cm pieces
3 tomatoes, seeded and chopped into 1 cm dice or 1 × 400 g can diced tomatoes
8 free-range or organic eggs
1 tablespoon cream
4 thin slices prosciutto
2 tablespoons parsley leaves, roughly chopped

1 Heat 1 tablespoon of the oil on a preheated flat grillplate or chargrill and fry the chorizo slices over medium heat for about 2–3 minutes on each side until brown. Transfer to a bowl and set aside.
2 Add the remaining oil to a frying pan and cook the onion and garlic over medium heat until they begin to brown. Turn the heat down to very low, add the capsicum and cook until it softens, for about 10–15 minutes. Add the tomatoes and cook for 5 minutes until the moisture is slightly reduced.
3 Break the eggs into a large mixing bowl and beat with a fork. Add the cream and season with salt and pepper. Make a well in the centre of the tomato mixture in the pan and pour in the eggs, allowing them to cook a little before folding them through. Fold through the reserved chorizo and remove from heat. Set aside.
4 Fry the prosciutto on a preheated flat grillplate or chargrill over high heat for about 1 minute until crisp.
5 Transfer the piperade to a single deep baking dish or four smaller dishes and top with the prosciutto and parsley.

Serves 4

Lobster, avocado and corn cocktail

PREP **15 mins**   COOK **15–20 mins**

You can substitute king prawns for the lobster here, but the lobby is something special when you want to spoil your friends.

The gazpacho dressing gives the recipe a nice sharp edge and cuts through the sweetness of the corn and the rich saltiness of the shellfish.

2 corn cobs (let's not put frozen corn with lobster)
1 desiree potato, chopped into 1½ cm dice
1 small (800 g–1 kg) cooked lobster
handful of lamb's lettuce or watercress sprigs,
 washed and dried
1 large avocado, peeled and diced
sea salt and freshly ground black pepper, to taste

DRESSING
1 large tomato, seeded and finely diced
½ Lebanese cucumber, peeled, seeded and finely diced
¼ red capsicum, white pith and seeds removed, diced
1 clove garlic, chopped
2 tablespoons extra virgin olive oil
1 tablespoon sherry vinegar
½ teaspoon Tabasco sauce
sea salt and freshly ground black pepper, to taste

1 To make the dressing, place all ingredients in a food processor and blend until smooth. Season to taste with salt and pepper. Reserve in fridge.
2 Bring a large saucepan of water to the boil, add the corn and cook, covered, for 10–15 minutes or until the corn is tender. Gently remove the corn from the pot and transfer to a plate. Once cool enough to handle, stand each corn cob up on a chopping board and carefully slice the kernels off with a large knife. Set kernels aside.
3 Boil the potato pieces in water in a small saucepan until they are just al dente – about 5 minutes. Allow to cool.
4 Carefully remove the meat from the lobster, cutting it into chunks of about 2 cm.
5 Arrange the greens and avocado in four cocktail glasses, scatter the potato and corn kernels over the top, then divide the lobster evenly between them. Spoon the dressing over each cocktail, and finish with a grind of pepper

Serves 4

Shellfish ceviche with coriander dressing

PREP **20 mins**   MARINATE **30 mins**

Ceviche, with its South American origins, is a splendid way of not cooking seafood.

Still with me? You use highly acidic citrus juice instead of heat to 'cook' the seafood, with the acid quickly turning the fish white and changing the texture dramatically. You don't want to eat a bucket of this, but a small serving is a great foil, with its lovely citrus sharpness, to a big lump of meat to follow.

CEVICHE
400 g green (raw) king prawns
200 g scallops, hard ligament removed,
  cut into ½ cm slices
50 ml tequila
½ teaspoon salt
⅔ cup (160 ml) lime juice (juice of about 2 limes)
½ red onion, finely diced
1 tomato, seeded and finely diced
½ red chilli, seeded and finely sliced
1 small cucumber, peeled, seeded and finely diced
½ teaspoon very finely grated lime zest
freshly ground black pepper, to taste

DRESSING
2 bunches coriander, leaves only
1 tablespoon lime juice
1 tablespoon extra virgin olive oil
1 teaspoon tequila

1 To prepare the prawns, twist off the head and carefully remove the shell. With a sharp knife, make a 5 mm-deep cut down the back, then remove the dark intestinal vein. Cut the prawns up into 1 cm pieces.
2 Combine tequila, salt and lime juice in a shallow glass or ceramic bowl and fold through the scallops and prawn pieces, turning to coat thoroughly. Cover bowl with plastic wrap and place in the fridge, giving the bowl a shake every 10 minutes or so to re-coat the shellfish. The shellfish should be opaque after half an hour.
3 To make the dressing, place leaves from 1½ bunches of coriander in a food processor, add the lime juice, olive oil and tequila and blend until smooth.
4 Drain the shellfish and add red onion, tomato, chilli, cucumber, lime zest and remaining coriander leaves. Mix well and transfer to four small plates, bowls or glasses.
5 Spoon dressing over the top and season with pepper. Serve immediately.

Serves 4

Smoked salmon and pumpernickel canapes with caraway seed butter

PREP **15 mins**

Denmark has come from nowhere in culinary terms to having the world's number one restaurant, so let's throw a few basic flavours from that neck of the woods together in some finger food.

You can buy ready-cut rounds or squares of pumpernickel from good delis and some supermarkets, otherwise it's no big deal to cut the slices into 3 cm squares.

about 20 × 3 cm rounds or squares of pumpernickel
100 g smoked salmon, cut into 2 cm slices
lemon, to serve

CARAWAY SEED BUTTER
1 teaspoon caraway seeds
150 g butter, cubed
1 teaspoon dill, finely chopped
1 teaspoon chives, finely chopped
½ teaspoon finely grated lemon zest
freshly ground black pepper, to taste

1 To make the butter, lightly crush the caraway seeds in a mortar and pestle. Combine butter, caraway seeds, dill, chives, lemon zest and pepper in a bowl and mash well with the back of a fork. You could also do this in a food processor, but then you'd have to wash it.
2 Spread the butter very generously onto the pumpernickel pieces and top each with a slice of smoked salmon, swirled around so it stands up. Serve with a little squeeze of lemon juice if you like.

Serves 4–6

Tomato and basil bruschetta >

PREP **10 mins**   MARINATE **20 mins**   COOK **2–4 mins**

With really ripe tomatoes, good olive oil and tasty bread, this can be an absolute joy. With ordinary, unripe tomatoes, cheap oil and crappy bread it will be an abomination. The simpler things are, the fewer places to hide bad produce.

I like to let the tomato mixture sit for a while to let the flavours develop.

6 very ripe tomatoes, seeded and finely diced
⅓ cup (80 ml) extra virgin olive oil
3 cloves garlic, 2 very finely chopped
about 12 basil leaves, torn
sea salt and freshly ground black pepper, to taste
4–6 slices rustic Italian bread, such as ciabatta (preferably stale), cut into 4–5 cm pieces

1 Mix together the tomatoes, olive oil, chopped garlic, basil, salt and pepper in a large bowl. Allow the mixture to sit for 20 minutes.
2 Grill the bread on a preheated chargrill for 1–2 minutes each side. Halve the remaining garlic clove and rub the cut side against what will be the top of each slice of bread. Spoon the tomato mixture on top and serve on a large serving plate as finger food.

Serves 4–6 and easily scales up to feed a party

34

< Buffalo mozzarella and heirloom tomato salad

PREP **10 mins**

I saw that very good, very funny London-based Italian chef, Giorgio Locatelli, a while ago on TV, talking about his homeland. He said that he saw a lot of buffalo mozzarella on menus, but not many buffalo anywhere. In Australia we can now get buffalo mozzarella locally or use the imported stuff, but I don't see many buffalo either.

I don't know about the flavour of the heirloom tomatoes that are now available, but they look terrific. All sorts of studies have been published saying tomatoes really do taste as good as they did years ago. Maybe tomatoes weren't that flash a generation ago after all?

400 g mixed heirloom tomatoes
120 ml extra virgin olive oil plus extra for drizzling
sea salt and freshly ground black pepper, to taste
300 g buffalo mozzarella
small handful basil leaves, torn

1 Slice the tomatoes and place them in a large bowl. Mix in the olive oil, salt and pepper, then divide between four small plates.
2 Roughly tear the cheese into bite-sized pieces and arrange on top of the tomatoes. Season with pepper and scatter with basil leaves.
3 Drizzle a tiny bit more oil over the top if you like.

Serves 4

Tuna carpaccio with lemon potato salad

PREP **15 mins**   COOK **8–10 mins**

I like the fact that this is a bit more of a meal than a couple of wafer-thin slices of fish – and these flavours really seem to work together.

It's a very nice starter before you eat your own body weight in red meat.

3 kipfler potatoes
300 g sashimi-quality tuna
4 sprigs dill, to serve

DRESSING
1 golden shallot, finely diced
rind from half a preserved lemon, finely sliced
1 heaped teaspoon tiny capers, rinsed
1 teaspoon dill, finely chopped
1 teaspoon chives, finely chopped
120 ml extra virgin olive oil
2 tablespoons lemon juice
sea salt and freshly ground black pepper, to taste

1 Steam or boil the potatoes for 8–10 minutes until just cooked. Allow to cool, then carefully peel them and cut them into half-centimetre slices.
2 To make the dressing, combine the shallot, lemon rind, capers, fresh herbs and half each of the oil and lemon juice in a large shallow bowl. Gently fold through the potato slices.
3 Slice the tuna as thinly as possible and arrange on four plates. Divide the salad evenly between the plates, then mix together the remaining oil and lemon juice and drizzle over the top. Season and serve immediately, decorating with a few sprigs of dill if you like.

Serves 4

COLD STARTERS

Oysters with three vinegar dressings

PREP **15 mins**

I was once served oysters with Limoncello dressing as finger food at a very new Sydney restaurant. Funnily enough, that restaurant closed a week or two later, after a scathing review which led to a long-running court battle. The moral of the story is not to put sweet dressings on oysters.

Here are a couple of very different ideas, using fragrant fresh herbs. Shoyu, used in the third dressing, is traditional Japanese soy sauce, aged in wooden casks for 18 months to two years. Unlike ordinary soy sauce, it has no artificial preservatives.

Each of these should be enough for a dozen oysters; you want the oyster to be the hero, not the dressings.

3 dozen oysters, preferably freshly shucked

TOMATO AND RED-WINE VINEGAR DRESSING
1 small tomato
4–6 drops Tabasco sauce, more to taste
1½ tablespoons red-wine vinegar
1 tablespoon extra virgin olive oil
12 chervil leaves

1 Make a little cross at the base of the tomato with a sharp knife and then place it in a saucepan of boiling water for 10–15 seconds. Transfer immediately to a bowl of iced water and then carefully remove the skin. Remove the seeds and dice the tomato.
2 Blend tomato, Tabasco sauce, vinegar and oil in a food processor until smooth, and spoon a little dressing over 12 oysters.

AGED BALSAMIC AND SHALLOT DRESSING
3 tablespoons aged balsamic vinegar
1 tablespoon extra virgin olive oil
1 tablespoon golden shallots (the little ones that look like they're wrapped in brown paper), very finely chopped
freshly ground black pepper, to taste
about 4 basil leaves, thinly sliced

1 Mix all ingredients except basil in a small jug.
2 Spoon a little dressing over 12 oysters, and scatter basil leaves over the top.

PICKLED GINGER AND RICE WINE VINEGAR DRESSING
1 tablespoon pickled ginger, very finely sliced
2 tablespoons Japanese rice vinegar
1 teaspoon shoyu (Japanese soy sauce)
12 coriander leaves

1 Mix all ingredients except coriander in a small jug.
2 Spoon a little dressing over the remaining 12 oysters, and scatter coriander leaves over the top.

Makes 36

Tuna sashimi and lychee cocktail

PREP 20 mins

Less is more of this big-flavoured starter; you really only want a few mouthfuls. What is surprising is just how easy this is to make, for such a flash result. Forget about sophistication, it's a simple treat if you have access to sashimi-quality tuna. Try to select the pieces without the pale white lines running through.

You can play with this as a concept. Avocado would work well in the mix, you could use salmon instead of tuna, and you could swap the lychees for a little nectarine or peach during the summer months.

100 ml pouring cream
1 teaspoon horseradish root, finely grated (more to taste)
4 fresh lychees, peeled and seeded
1 lime
1 small cucumber, peeled, seeded and finely diced
1 teaspoon extra virgin olive oil
½ cup iceberg lettuce, very finely shredded
150 g sashimi-quality tuna cut into 1 cm cubes
freshly ground black pepper to taste
2 basil leaves, torn

1 Whip cream until quite firm then fold through horseradish. Taste and add more if required. Reserve, covered, in the fridge.
2 Cut the lychees into 1 cm pieces – you should get about four to eight pieces from each lychee. Peel the lime, then cut along the white membrane so that you have only the fruit segments. Cut these in half. Place lychees, lime segments and cucumber in a small bowl, add the olive oil and squeeze the juice from what is left of the lime. Mix well.
3 Divide the lettuce evenly between four small cocktail glasses or large shot glasses. Place a teaspoon of the lychee mixture in each glass, then a quarter of the tuna, then a little more of the lychee mixture (the tuna isn't mixed through or the lime would 'cook' it as in the ceviche on page 32).
4 Serve topped with a teaspoon of the horseradish cream, a grind of pepper and a little basil.

Serves 4

Moreton Bay bug panzanella salad >

PREP 15 mins   COOK 20–30 mins

There's your lovely plain peasant dish of stale bread and tomato salad with some basil, all swimming in good olive oil and balsamic. Then there's the also-lovely panzanella – a chopped salad with tomatoes, cucumber, onion, croutons, and often green capsicum and goat's cheese as well these days.

Just about anything tastes better with shellfish, so let's skip the cheese and add some crustacean flavours. For a bit of variety, you could use prawns, lobster or crabmeat instead of bugs.

2 slices day-old sourdough bread, cut into 1½–2 cm cubes
6 cooked Moreton Bay bugs or Balmain bugs
1 red onion, peeled and finely sliced
2 tomatoes, seeded and chopped into 1 cm dice
1 cucumber, peeled, seeded and finely diced
½ bulb fennel, core discarded, very finely sliced
2 tablespoons flat-leaf parsley leaves, roughly chopped
10 basil leaves, torn

DRESSING
½ cup (125 ml) extra virgin olive oil
¼ cup (60 ml) lemon juice (juice of 1 lemon)
1 clove garlic, crushed
sea salt and freshly ground black pepper, to taste

1 Preheat the oven to 120°C. Place the bread cubes on an oven tray lined with baking paper and bake them for 20–30 minutes until they dry out and just start to colour. You could also do this on your barbecue.
2 Carefully remove the meat from the bugs, cutting it into nice big chunks, and place on a plate in the fridge. If the bugs are small, you could leave the tails intact.
3 To make the dressing, mix together all ingredients in a large salad bowl. Toss through the bread, onion, tomatoes, cucumber, fennel and fresh herbs, mixing well, then mix in the bug meat.

Serves 4

Shellfish guacamole dip

PREP 15 mins

A good guacamole is a fine thing in its own right. Spicy, smooth, crunchy, limey, sour – all at the same time. The addition of some good shellfish just makes it all the more interesting and delicious. It goes from a nibble to a starter of sorts.

2 ripe avocados, peeled
1 red onion, finely diced
1 tomato, seeded and finely diced
½ cucumber, peeled, seeded and finely diced
2 tablespoons olive oil
1 tablespoon lime juice
2 tablespoons coriander leaves, finely chopped
100 g cooked prawns chopped into 1 cm pieces
    or crabmeat, or mixture of both
½ teaspoon Tabasco sauce
sea salt and freshly ground black pepper, to taste
organic corn chips or toasted baguette slices

1 Chop or lightly mash avocados with a fork and transfer to serving bowl. Mix in the rest of the ingredients and serve with corn chips or baguette.

Serves 4–6 as a snack

Daggy devilled eggs >

PREP 15 mins   COOK 5 mins

I'm allowed one or two daggy retro dishes. This takes me back to Mum and Dad's early '60s show-off canapes of Jatz crackers, Kraft processed cheese and nuclear-power-station-red pickled onions – yum.

You can be posh and pipe the filling in (like I have to do for a cookbook), or just bung it in with a teaspoon (like I'd do at home).

Daggy but delicious.

12 large free-range or organic eggs
2 tablespoons best-quality mayonnaise
1 tablespoon olive oil
1 tablespoon Dijon mustard
1 tablespoon white-wine vinegar
¼–½ teaspoon Tabasco sauce, to taste
sea salt and freshly ground white pepper, to taste
1 tablespoon chives, finely chopped
1 teaspoon paprika, to serve

1 Put the eggs in cold water in a small saucepan, bring to the boil, then simmer for 5 minutes. Rinse immediately under cold water. Once the eggs have cooled, peel them, then cut them in half and carefully remove the yolks, leaving the eggwhites intact and setting them aside.
2 Reserving the eggwhites, place the yolks and all other ingredients except the paprika in a food processor and blend to a smooth paste – or do it in a bowl with a fork, and save washing-up. Fold through the chives.
3 Pipe or spoon the egg yolk mixture into the space in the eggwhites where the yolk used to be and dust with a tiny amount of paprika.

Serves 6–12

< Nicoise salad

PREP 15 mins   COOK 15 mins

Potatoes, no potatoes? Capsicum, no capsicum?
Capers, no capers? The purists find it hard to agree
on what really should go into a classic Nicoise. I did
one with a slab of grilled tuna as a main course in my
first book, *The Great Aussie Barbie Cookbook,* but
here's my version of the classic.

Never a side dish, this is a perfect starter before
a piece of barbecued meat.

8 small new potatoes
4 free-range or organic eggs
500 g green beans
4 tomatoes
1 clove garlic, cut in half
6–8 cos or baby cos lettuce leaves
20 small black olives
about 8 basil leaves, torn
200 g best-quality canned tuna in oil
8 anchovy fillets

DRESSING
120 ml extra virgin olive oil
2 tablespoons white-wine vinegar
1 tablespoon lemon juice
sea salt and freshly ground pepper to taste
½ teaspoon Dijon mustard
1 heaped teaspoon shallot, finely chopped

1 Steam or boil the potatoes for 8–10 minutes until just
  cooked, then cut in half and reserve.
2 Put the eggs in cold water in a small saucepan, bring to
  the boil, then simmer for 5 minutes. Rinse immediately
  under cold water. Once the eggs have cooled, peel and
  quarter them.
3 Steam or boil the green beans for 2 minutes and refresh
  in iced water to maintain their colour and stop them from
  cooking more.
4 Cut each tomato into 6 or 8 pieces.
5 Rub the inside of a large salad bowl with the garlic clove
  then discard it. To make the dressing, mix together the
  dressing ingredients in the bowl. Gently toss through the
  potatoes, boiled eggs, beans, tomatoes, lettuce, olives
  and basil, mixing well.
6 Break the tuna into the bowl and mix it in with the other
  ingredients. Arrange anchovies on top.

Serves 4

Veal fillet with burrata

PREP 10 mins   COOK 4–6 mins   REST 10 mins

You might have to hunt to find real, tiny pink veal fillets,
but they're worth the effort.

Burrata is a very creamy cow's milk cheese, sort of
a super-premium mozzarella, which is now being
produced locally as well as being imported from Italy.
You should be able to find it at specialty food stores,
but substitute buffalo mozzarella if you can't find it.

Packaged walnuts will do if you can't find fresh.

Mixed together, these high-quality ingredients make
a pretty special sort of salad.

2–4 veal fillets, 100–150 g each
1 tablespoon olive oil
sea salt and freshly ground black pepper, to taste
200 g burrata cheese, sliced
2 witlof
1 cup (120 g) walnut halves
½ cup flat-leaf parsley leaves, finely chopped
200 g burrata cheese, sliced

DRESSING
1 tablespoon walnut oil (substitute extra virgin olive oil)
½ tablespoon white-wine vinegar
sea salt and freshly ground black pepper, to taste

1 Brush the veal with the olive oil and season with salt and
  pepper. Cook on a preheated flat grillplate over medium
  heat for about 2–3 minutes on each side until rare to
  medium–rare. Rest for 10 minutes, then refrigerate,
  covered, until ready to use.
2 To make the dressing, combine the walnut oil and vinegar in
  a large salad bowl with salt and pepper. Gently toss through
  the witlof, parsley and walnuts, then arrange the burrata
  slices on top.
3 Slice the veal thinly and arrange on a plate or in the bowl
  with the burrata and witlof salad.

Serves 6

COLD STARTERS

Smoked salmon, watercress and avocado salad with caper dressing

PREP 15 mins   COOK 2 mins

If I were a sexist kind of guy – which of course I'm not – I would describe this as 'girl food'. Nice and light, plenty of green things and no big lump of red meat involved.

What is in no way sugar and spice and all things nice is the gutsy dressing of garlic, anchovies, capers and mustard that really gives this dish some oomph.

8 green beans
1 cucumber, peeled, seeded and sliced
1 large avocado, peeled and diced
2–3 loosely packed cups picked watercress leaves
  (tough stems discarded)
8 slices smoked salmon
lime wedges

DRESSING
1 clove garlic, chopped
2 anchovy fillets
1 tablespoon salted capers, thoroughly rinsed
1 teaspoon Dijon mustard
2 tablespoons olive oil
1 tablespoon lime juice
sea salt and freshly ground black pepper, to taste
1 tablespoon chives, chopped

1 Steam or boil the green beans for 2 minutes then refresh them in iced water to maintain their colour and stop them from cooking more. Cut into 2 cm lengths and set aside.
2 To make the dressing, combine all ingredients except the chives in a food processor and blend until smooth, then stir through the chives.
3 Transfer all but one tablespoon of dressing to a large bowl and gently toss through the beans, cucumber, avocado and watercress.
4 Divide the salad evenly between four plates and top with smoked salmon slices and lime wedges, then drizzle over remaining dressing.

Serves 4

Kingfish carpaccio with fennel and preserved lemon >

PREP 15 mins   COOK 5 mins

I'm so over the Italian restaurant version of carpaccio, where they freeze the fish and slice it paper-thin with an electric slicer – it seems to taste of nothing much.

I much prefer thicker, hand-cut pieces of fish, sometimes called crudo, especially with the grown-up flavours of the pickled fennel and preserved lemon accompaniment.

You can be a bit restaurant-y and serve it on chilled plates, or go the rustic route as in the photo opposite.

¾ cup (180 ml) white-wine vinegar
6 whole cloves
1 small fennel bulb, hard core removed, finely sliced, fronds reserved
1 heaped teaspoon capers (rinsed if in salt), chopped
1 tablespoon preserved lemon rind, finely diced
½ cup (125 ml) extra virgin olive oil
200 g sashimi-quality kingfish
freshly ground black pepper, to taste
thinly sliced baguette, to serve (optional)

1 If serving on plates chill four plates in the fridge.
2 Place the vinegar and cloves in a small saucepan and bring to the boil. Add the sliced fennel, stirring to immerse it and bring to the boil again, then simmer for 1 minute. Remove the pan from the heat to cool.
3 Drain the pan, reserving the fennel and discarding the cloves. Combine the fennel, capers, preserved lemon and olive oil in a bowl. Chop the reserved fennel fronds and add them to the mix, stirring well to combine. Allow the flavours to develop for a few minutes.
4 Slice the kingfish thinly and divide it evenly between the chilled plates or arrange on a wooden board. Spoon the fennel and lemon mixture over, completely covering the fish.
5 Season with pepper and serve with baguette if you like.

Serves 4

46

HOT
STARTERS

'Back-to-front' marinated prawns

PREP 10 mins   COOK 5 mins   REST 5 mins

The 'Back-to-front' Steak recipe (see page 89) is just about my favourite barbecue dish. I really like the way the marinade flavours the meat after it's cooked. We're doing exactly the same thing here with prawns and it works just as well.

12 large green (raw) king prawns
3 cloves garlic, crushed
3 tablespoons olive oil plus an additional ½ cup (125 ml) olive oil
1 tablespoon rosemary leaves, finely chopped
½ teaspoon dried chilli flakes (optional)
2 tablespoons lemon juice
1 teaspoon finely grated lemon zest
sea salt and freshly ground black pepper, to taste
baguette or crusty bread, to serve

1 To prepare the prawns, twist off the head and carefully remove the shell. With a sharp knife, make a 5 mm-deep cut down the back, then remove the dark intestinal vein, leaving the last section of tail on if you like.
2 In a shallow, heatproof dish, gently cook the garlic in two tablespoons of olive oil over medium heat and add the rosemary and chilli (if using). Add the ½ cup of olive oil, lemon juice and zest and warm through for 1 minute, not allowing the mixture to boil or get too hot. Remove from the heat.
3 Brush the prawns with the last tablespoon of olive oil and season well with salt and pepper. Cook them on a preheated chargrill over medium–high heat until they are just firm to the touch and opaque.
4 Add the prawns to the warm oil and lemon mixture, mixing thoroughly to make sure they are well coated. Cover loosely with foil for 5 minutes before serving with crusty bread.

Serves 4

Moroccan scallop skewers >

PREP 10 mins   COOK 2–3 mins

Less is much, much more when it comes to cooking these. You definitely want the centre of the scallops warm, but translucent.

You need to offer these around quickly as the scallops will be delicate, rich and delicious straight from the grill, but tough and dry when they've sat for 10 minutes.

Very few scallops won't have been frozen, but make sure you avoid those sitting in a puddle of water in fish shop windows. We now get good imports from Japan, US, Canada, Chile and even Russia, as well as great local products from Queensland and South Australia.

12 plump white scallops, hard sinew trimmed off
1 tablespoon olive oil
1 teaspoon ras el hanout
1 tablespoon cumin seeds
1 teaspoon ground coriander
1 teaspoon paprika (not smoked)
¼ teaspoon cayenne pepper or chilli powder (optional)
sea salt and freshly ground black pepper, to taste
lime wedges to serve

1 Place the scallops in a bowl with the oil and gently stir to coat.
2 Place all other ingredients except lime in a plastic bag or shallow glass or ceramic bowl and mix well. Add the scallops and shake the bag or mix thoroughly in the bowl until the scallops are well coated.
3 Thread three scallops on each skewer, then cook on a lightly oiled preheated chargrill over high heat for no more than a minute each side, so that the outside is brown and the inside is rare to medium–rare.
4 Sprinkle with a little sea salt and pepper and serve immediately with lime wedges.

Serves 4

HOT STARTERS

Asian-spiced quail with cucumber dipping sauce

PREP **15 mins**   MARINATE **2–4 hrs**   COOK **10–15 mins**   REST **5 mins**

No genius here, just some nice Asian flavours to go with these yummy little birds, which cook so quickly on the barbecue. I really like the way the fresh cucumber salad works with the Asian marinade flavours.

6 butterflied quail (you could ask your
   poultry supplier to do this)
1 tablespoon sea salt
½ teaspoon five-spice
½ tablespoon Sichuan pepper

MARINADE
1 tablespoon sesame oil
1 tablespoon neutral oil
2 tablespoons mirin
1 teaspoon rice vinegar
2 tablespoons soy sauce
2 cloves garlic, grated
small thumb ginger, grated

CUCUMBER DIPPING SAUCE
½ small cucumber, peeled, seeded and
   cut into ½ cm dice
½ cup (125 ml) lime juice
1 tablespoon fish sauce
2 tablespoons cold water
1 bird's eye or red chilli, seeded and finely sliced
1 teaspoon caster sugar
pinch of salt
pinch of white pepper

1 To butterfly the quail yourself, use a sharp knife to cut through the cavity on either side of the backbone, discard the backbone, then flatten the bird out with a heavy knife.
2 Combine the marinade ingredients in a shallow glass or ceramic bowl and add the quail, turning to coat thoroughly. Cover with plastic film and leave in the fridge to marinate for 2–4 hours.
3 To make the sauce, combine all ingredients in a bowl and stir to dissolve sugar. Taste to see if it needs more lime juice, fish sauce or sugar for balance. Set aside.
4 Remove the quail from the marinade and dry with a paper towel. Grind the salt, five-spice and Sichuan pepper together with a mortar and pestle, and sprinkle over both sides of the quail.
5 Cook on a preheated chargrill over medium–hot heat for about 5–7 minutes on each side until just cooked through. Rest, loosely covered, for 5 minutes before serving.
6 Serve quail with dipping sauce.

Serves 6

< Prawns with sage and pancetta

PREP 15 mins   COOK 5 mins

If you're planning a festive barbecue, nothing beats a well-cooked steak as a main course (have a snoop at my website www.aussiebarbie.com.au for videos and tips on how to do that).

But as a delicious and really quick starter, these prawns are terrific. You can make them before your guests arrive and keep them in the fridge, covered with plastic wrap.

12 green (raw) king prawns
12 sage leaves
12 thin slices pancetta (not the spicy one)
lemon halves, to serve
baby rocket leaves, to serve (optional)

1 To prepare the prawns, twist off the head and carefully remove the shell. With a sharp knife, make a 5 mm-deep cut down the back, then remove the dark intestinal vein, placing a sage leaf into the cavity. Leave the last section of tail on.
2 Wrap each prawn in a slice of pancetta. Cook on a preheated flat grillplate over medium–high heat until the prawns are just firm to the touch and opaque, and the pancetta is crisp.
3 Serve immediately with lemon halves and maybe some dressed baby rocket leaves.

Serves 4

Crab cakes

PREP 15 mins   COOK 10–15 mins

These are a bit elegant (and expensive if you use good-quality crabmeat, available from fish shops and markets) for an everyday barbecue, but it is nice to have something up your sleeve for a special occasion. Don't tell anyone, but you can also cook them on a regular stove in the kitchen. Great served with Herb Aioli (see page 84), Tzatziki Salad (see page 106) or Tartare Sauce (see page 148).

1 small onion, very finely chopped
1 clove garlic, crushed or finely chopped
1 tablespoon butter
250 g crabmeat (cooked)
2 cups (140 g) stale white breadcrumbs
2 free-range or organic eggs
2 tablespoons coriander leaves, finely chopped
sea salt and freshly ground black pepper, to taste
½ cup (125 ml) neutral oil for frying
lemon wedges, to serve
Tartare Sauce, to serve (see page 148)

1 Fry the onion and garlic in butter in a small pan over medium heat until soft. Allow to cool.
2 Combine onion and garlic mixture, crabmeat, breadcrumbs, eggs and coriander in a large bowl and mix well. Season with salt and pepper. Form the mixture into walnut-sized balls and flatten into patty shapes.
3 Cook the crab cakes in a little oil on a preheated flat grillplate over medium heat for 2–3 minutes on each side until golden-brown.
4 Serve with lemon wedges and tartare sauce.

Serves 4

HOT STARTERS

Salt and pepper scallops

PREP 10 mins   COOK 2–3 mins

Salt and pepper house brick would probably taste OK. The salt and Sichuan pepper coating works so well on calamari, soft shell crab, prawns, tofu, even pieces of pork.

I tried it with scallops one day and then cooked it at my Boys Can Cook School to rave reviews, so here it is.

Try to get nice big, meaty scallops for this, and make sure they've been very well drained, or the oil will spit like crazy.

⅓ cup (80 ml) lemon juice
2 teaspoons white pepper
1 teaspoon salt
12–16 plump scallops, hard ligament removed
1 free-range or organic eggwhite
1 tablespoon sea salt
1 cup (150 g) potato starch or tapioca flour
½ tablespoon ground Sichuan pepper
½ teaspoon five-spice powder
½ cup (125 ml) neutral oil for frying

1 Combine the lemon juice, white pepper and 1 teaspoon of salt in a bowl and mix well. Transfer to four small dipping bowls or drizzle over the scallops when cooked.
2 Beat the eggwhite until soft peaks form. Combine the salt, potato starch, pepper and five-spice powder in a separate bowl. Dip the scallops into the eggwhite, then coat well with the spice mixture.
3 Pour the oil onto a preheated flat grillplate and cook scallops over high heat for about 1 minute each side, so that they are medium–rare, and still translucent in the middle. Drain well on paper towel.
4 Place on four small plates and serve with dipping sauce.

Serves 4

Honey, lime and dukkah-crusted king prawns >

PREP 15 mins   COOK 10 mins

Some lovely big flavours here with king prawns, honey, lime and that fabulous dukkah blend, which is a dry mix of roasted nuts, seeds and spices. By all means, make your own (see recipe on page 99) or buy it from a spice shop like Herbie's.

12–16 green (raw) king prawns
⅓ cup (80 ml) honey
zest and juice of 1 lime
2 tablespoons neutral oil
1 cup dukkah mix (see recipe page 99)
additional lime halves, to serve
salad greens, to serve (optional)

1 To prepare the prawns, twist off the head and carefully remove the shell. With a sharp knife, make a 5 mm-deep cut down the back, then remove the dark intestinal vein, leaving the last section of tail on if you like. Set aside somewhere cool.
2 Place honey, lime zest and juice and 1 tablespoon of water in a small saucepan and heat gently, stirring until the honey dissolves. Pour the warm honey and lime mixture into a bowl next to a plate with the dukkah blend on it.
3 Brush the prawns with oil then cook them on a preheated flat grillplate or chargrill over medium–high heat until they are just firm to the touch and opaque.
4 When the prawns are cooked, pick them up by their tails and dip them in the honey and lime mixture, then roll them in the dukkah blend until they are well coated.
5 Quickly arrange them on plates and serve with salad greens and lime halves if you like.

Serves 4

Grilled garlic pine mushrooms

PREP 5 mins COOK 3–4 mins

There's something very special about pine mushrooms that makes me want to buy them every time I see them in specialty fruit and veg shops – I worry that they'll disappear for another year the next day.

Of course you could use densely flavoured portobellos or even field mushrooms, but they won't have that amazing orange colour, firm texture or unique earthy flavour that the pine mushrooms do. For me, it's all about lightly complementing their flavour, rather than dominating it, so just a little garlic, oil and parsley and maybe just a hint of chilli.

2 cloves garlic, crushed
½ cup (125 ml) olive oil
¼ teaspoon chilli flakes
1 tablespoon flat-leaf parsley leaves, finely chopped
sea salt and freshly ground black pepper, to taste
12–16 pine mushrooms, stalks cut level with underside, dirt and grass removed with a brush or a paper towel (never wash them)
sea salt, to serve

1 Combine all ingredients except the mushrooms in a small bowl and mix well.
2 Cook the mushrooms on a preheated chargrill, over high heat, underside down, for about 1 minute.
3 Turn the mushrooms over and spoon or brush the oil mixture onto their underside, cooking the top side for another minute or so. The mushrooms should still be quite firm, not limp.
4 Transfer to four small plates and serve just as they are, maybe with a little sea salt.

Serves 4

Prosciutto-wrapped asparagus with lime mayonnaise >

PREP 15 mins COOK 3–5 mins

The saltiness of the prosciutto works very nicely with the herbaceousness of the asparagus and the sweetness of the mayo in this very simple dish. Don't make it in February and March, when most asparagus is imported. It works best with the really thick asparagus from Victoria available in spring and summer.

The mayo is also great with white fish, salmon or ocean trout but not with very oily, dense fish. You could just add the lime to best-quality store-bought mayo if you like.

12 thick spears asparagus, woody stalks trimmed off
6 thin slices of prosciutto, cut in half

LIME MAYONNAISE
2 free-range or organic egg yolks
½ teaspoon Dijon mustard
150 ml extra virgin olive oil
100 ml peanut oil
finely grated zest of one lime
1 tablespoon lime juice

1 To make the lime mayonnaise, place the egg yolks and Dijon mustard in a large bowl. Add the olive oil and peanut oil in the thinnest possible stream, whisking vigorously with a wire whisk or fork until the mixture thickens. Whisk through the lime zest and juice and refrigerate until ready to use.
2 Wrap a slice of prosciutto around each spear of asparagus, then grill the asparagus on a preheated chargrill over high heat for a few minutes, turning regularly until the prosciutto begins to crisp.
3 Serve with lime mayonnaise.

Serves 4

HOT STARTERS

< Lamb and oregano meatballs

PREP 15 mins   COOK 5–7 mins

You won't be able to make enough of these for your friends, and they're also pretty handy cold from the fridge the next day if a nasty hangover has snuck up on you – as happens. Panko crumbs are a Japanese ingredient, and they are closer to flakes than crumbs, so they are larger than ordinary breadcrumbs and tend to have a better flavour and texture. I realise that this is a Japanese ingredient in an essentially Greek dish, but hey, this is Australia and anything goes.

750 g lamb mince
2 free-range or organic egg yolks
1 tablespoon dried oregano leaves
1 cup (100g) panko breadcrumbs
finely grated zest of one lemon
1 teaspoon salt
½ teaspoon freshly ground black pepper
½ cup (125 ml) olive or neutral oil
sea salt, to serve
lemon wedges, to serve

1 Combine lamb mince, egg yolks, oregano, breadcrumbs, lemon zest, salt and pepper in a large bowl and mix very thoroughly with your hands. Roll mixture into walnut-size meatballs or, if you prefer, shape it into rissoles.
2 Cook the meatballs in the oil on a preheated flat grillplate over medium heat for about 5–7 minutes, turning regularly so that they cook through without burning.
3 Serve with a sprinkle of sea salt and lemon wedges.

Serves 4 as a starter, plenty more as a snack

Bacon-wrapped dates

PREP 10 mins   COOK 5 mins

These are really more-ish and a bit different for a barbecue snack, and they only take a minute or two to sort.
   Try to find streaky bacon; that is, not the meaty eye part. You could always revert to the much trendier pancetta, but who wants to be trendy?

12 dried dates
1 heaped teaspoon brown sugar
12 whole unsalted almonds
6 thin rashers streaky rindless bacon,
   or 12 thin slices pancetta
1 tablespoon balsamic vinegar, to serve
freshly ground black pepper, to serve

1 Make a small incision in each date with a sharp knife and squeeze out the seed. Insert an almond with a little sugar in its place, and wrap with enough bacon or pancetta to go around at least one and a half times. Secure with a toothpick.
2 Cook on a preheated chargrill or flat grillplate over medium–hot heat for about 2 minutes on each side, until the bacon is cooked.
3 To serve, remove toothpicks, place on a plate, drizzle with balsamic vinegar and finish with a grind of pepper.

Serves 4 as a starter, 6–12 as a snack

HOT STARTERS

Grilled figs in prosciutto with gorgonzola sauce

PREP 10 mins   COOK 10 mins

My mate Armando Percuoco's famous dish of figs wrapped in prosciutto and baked with dolce gorgonzola, cream and a little butter must be one of the most imitated in Australia. The three main ingredients seem to pop up cooked or raw everywhere from pub dining rooms to swank canapes.

Armando generously let me adapt it for *The Great Aussie Bloke's Cookbook* and the same flavours work gangbusters on the barbie.

300 ml cream
100 g gorgonzola dolce cheese
25 g butter
12 very thin slices prosciutto
6 figs, halved
freshly ground black pepper, to serve (optional)
2 tablespoons parsley, chopped, to serve (optional)

1 Combine cream, gorgonzola and butter in a saucepan and stir over low heat for a couple of minutes until the cheese melts into the cream. Set aside.
2 Wrap a slice of prosciutto around each fig half. Cook on a preheated chargrill over very high heat for about 1 minute on each side. (You shouldn't need any oil because of the fat in the prosciutto, and you're not trying to cook the figs, just warm them).
3 To serve, arrange three fig halves on each plate and spoon over the sauce. If you like, grate a little pepper and sprinkle some very finely chopped parsley on top.

Serves 4

Jerk chicken wings >

PREP 15 mins   MARINATE 4–12 hrs   COOK 20 mins

Best keep these away from the kiddies or they'll burn their tongues on these spicy, flavour-packed treats. You might too, but you'll have icy-cold beer to soothe the heat. Just apply more jerk wings then more beer and repeat the process.

You can make these as hot as you like, by upping the quantity of fresh chillies and Tabasco. I don't like them too hot, myself; I think it's better to be able to taste the other flavours.

24 mid wing portions of chicken (not the wing 'drumstick' and not the wing tip)
lime halves

MARINADE
3–4 jalapeno (or scotch bonnet, to really spice things up) chillies, seeded and finely chopped
6 spring onions, white and pale-green parts only, finely sliced
4 cloves garlic, crushed
2 tablespoons fresh orange juice
1 teaspoon finely grated orange zest
1 teaspoon salt
½ teaspoon Tabasco sauce
2 teaspoons ground allspice
1 teaspoon ground thyme
½ teaspoon ground cinnamon
½ teaspoon ground nutmeg
½ teaspoon freshly ground black pepper
2 tablespoons neutral oil

1 To make the marinade, combine all ingredients in a food processor and mix well.
2 Combine the marinade ingredients in a shallow glass or ceramic bowl and add the chicken wings, turning to coat thoroughly. Cover with plastic film and leave in the fridge to marinate for 4–12 hours.
3 Remove the chicken wings from the marinade and dry with paper towel. Cook on preheated chargrill or flat grillplate over low–medium heat for about 20 minutes, turning occasionally.
4 Serve with lime halves and icy cold beer, as this isn't a very wine-friendly dish.

Serves 4–6

HOT STARTERS

Garlic prawns

PREP 15 mins   MARINATE 2–4 hrs   COOK 4–6 mins

If you're old enough, you'll remember these being trotted out in every Italian restaurant, French so-called bistro and, I'm guessing, what were called 'continental' restaurants before that.

The fact is there's nothing wrong with them – they're bloody fantastic. It's just nice to have a few other things to choose from these days.

16–20 green (raw) king prawns
4 cloves garlic, chopped
¼ teaspoon chilli flakes
1 tablespoon parsley leaves, roughly chopped
1 cup (250 ml) olive oil
½ teaspoon sea salt
½ teaspoon freshly ground black pepper, to taste
lemon wedges, to serve

1 To prepare the prawns, twist off the head and carefully remove the shell. With a sharp knife, make a 5 mm-deep cut down the back, then remove the dark intestinal vein, leaving the last section of tail on if you like.
2 Combine garlic, chilli flakes, parsley, oil, salt and pepper in a food processor and blend well.
3 Pour the garlic mixture into a shallow glass or ceramic bowl and add the prawns, turning to coat thoroughly. Cover with plastic film and leave in the fridge to marinate for 2–4 hours.
4 Remove prawns from fridge and cook them on a preheated flat grillplate over medium–high heat for about 2–3 minutes each side until the prawns are just firm to the touch and opaque.
5 Serve with lemon wedges.

Serves 4 as a starter, more as finger food

Easy seafood salad >

PREP 15 mins   COOK 15–20 mins

Sometimes you're not showing off, not trying to impress or do anything cutting edge. This is one of those times, with what is almost an '80s combination of lovely simple ingredients. Just bloody delicious.

1 red capsicum, white insides and seeds removed, cut into 1 cm strips
⅓ cup (80 ml) extra virgin olive oil
1 tablespoon slivered almonds
16 green (raw) king prawns
12 white scallops, hard sinew removed
1 small frisee lettuce
1 avocado, peeled, stone removed and diced
8 cherry tomatoes, halved

DRESSING
⅓ cup (80 ml) extra virgin olive oil
2 tablespoons lemon juice
sea salt and freshly ground pepper, to taste

1 Gently cook the capsicum in half of the oil on a preheated flat grillplate over low heat until it softens. Set aside.
2 Toast the almonds, by placing them in a dry frying pan over medium heat and shake them regularly until they brown. Set aside.
3 To prepare the prawns, twist off the head and carefully remove the shell. With a sharp knife, make a 5 mm-deep cut down the back, then remove the dark intestinal vein, leaving the last section of tail on if you like.
4 Cook the prawns and scallops in the other half of the oil on a preheated flat grillplate over medium–high heat. Cook the scallops for about 1 minute each side, until they are translucent, and the prawns for about 2–3 minutes each side until they are just firm to the touch and opaque. Reserve in a shallow bowl. If you're a multi-tasker, the seafood can go onto the barbie as the capsicum is nearly done.
5 To make the dressing, mix together the oil, lemon juice, salt and pepper in the base of a large salad bowl. Toss through the frisee, mixing well.
6 To serve, arrange the frisee on four small plates, then place the seafood, avocado, tomatoes and capsicum on top. Spoon over any juices from the seafood and the remaining salad dressing. Scatter slivered almonds on top.

Serves 4

< Prawn and pineapple skewers with black pepper butter sauce

PREP 15 mins   COOK 15–20 mins

I like the way the sweetness and pepper hit of the sauce work with the pineapple in this recipe. If you're not a pineapple fan, just cook a pile of prawns.

The sauce is just a twist on a French beurre blanc, which sounds flash but just means reducing wine, vinegar and some other flavours down to their essence and throwing in some butter.

16 green (raw) king prawns
½ pineapple, peeled and cut into 2 cm × 4 cm pieces
2 tablespoons neutral oil

SAUCE
1 cup (250 ml) dry white wine
½ cup (125 ml) white-wine vinegar
1 vanilla bean, split
1 shallot, chopped
⅓ cup (80 ml) dark rum
1 teaspoon freshly ground black pepper
sea salt, to taste
125 g cold butter, cut into 1–2 cm cubes

1 To prepare the prawns, twist off the head and carefully remove the shell. With a sharp knife, make a 5 mm-deep cut down the back, then remove the dark intestinal vein, leaving the last section of tail on if you like.
2 Thread the prawns and pineapple pieces onto four skewers and keep somewhere cool until ready to cook.
3 Place the wine, vinegar, vanilla bean and shallot in a saucepan and bring to the boil, then simmer and reduce the liquid to about one-half. Add the rum and reduce until only 2 tablespoons of liquid are left. Carefully remove the solids with a slotted spoon and add pepper.
4 Brush the skewers with oil, season with small amount of salt and cook on a preheated chargrill over high heat until the prawns are just firm to the touch and opaque.
5 While you are cooking the prawn skewers, reheat the liquid in the saucepan over medium heat and, when hot, remove from the heat and stir through the cold butter until the sauce is well-blended.
6 To serve, place the skewers on four plates and spoon over the butter sauce.

Serves 4

Thai-style corn and prawn fritters

PREP 15 mins   COOK 20 mins

These can be a starter or great finger food. You can ramp up the chilli if that's your inclination and put the fire out with cold beers if that's your inclination.

200 g green (raw) prawns
1½ corn cobs, or 1½ cups (240 g) frozen corn kernels
½ red chilli, very finely chopped (optional)
100 g plain flour or tapioca flour
2 spring onions, white and pale-green parts only, finely chopped
2 free-range or organic eggs
1 clove garlic, chopped
1 tablespoon Thai red curry paste
1 tablespoon fish sauce
1 teaspoon palm sugar or white sugar
½ cup (125 ml) neutral oil for frying
sweet chilli sauce, to serve
lime wedges, to serve

1 To prepare the prawns, twist off the head and carefully remove the shell. With a sharp knife, make a 5 mm-deep cut down the back, then remove the dark intestinal vein. Remove all tails, and chop prawns into 1 cm pieces and set aside somewhere cool.
2 Bring a large saucepan of water to the boil, add the corn and cook, covered, for 10–15 minutes or until the corn is tender. Gently remove the corn from the pot and transfer to a plate. Once cool enough to handle, stand each corn cob up on a chopping board and carefully slice the kernels off with a large knife.
3 Combine half the prawns and half the corn kernels (reserving the rest of both) with all other ingredients (except the chilli, if using, and the oil) in a food processor and blend to a smooth paste.
4 Transfer mixture to a bowl and fold through the reserved corn kernels, prawns and chilli, if using, mixing well.
5 Shape mixture into small, quite flat fritters. Cook fritters in the oil on a preheated flat grillplate over medium–high heat for about 2–3 minutes on each side until golden-brown and cooked through.
6 Serve with sweet chilli sauce or lime wedges.

Serves 4–6

HOT STARTERS

Kimbo's perfect steak and bangers

STEAK COOK **10 mins**   REST **5–10 mins**   **SAUSAGES** COOK **15 mins**   REST **5 mins**

I'd like a dollar for every time I have gone through what I reckon are the steps to cooking the perfect steak and sausages on TV, radio and in I don't know how many cooking classes.

To me, it's all just common sense. But I never cease to be amazed by guys who manage to incinerate good steaks and bangers – and then present them proudly as if they are the result of a combination of genius and heroic effort.

THE PERFECT STEAK
Let's stick with the common sense thought.

- Buy the BEST STEAK that you can afford. Just because 'it's only a barbecue' doesn't mean that you should eat ordinary meat.
- If you want a rare or even medium–rare steak, it should be THICK enough to stay rare or pink in the middle in the time it takes to get the outside nicely browned and caramelised. Conversely, if you want a well-done steak, it should be THIN enough that it won't burn on the outside while the inside is cooking right through.
- If you get any steak out of the fridge and throw it straight on the barbie, it won't cook evenly. Bring your steak back to ROOM TEMPERATURE for half an hour to an hour (not in the blazing sun) before you cook it.
- I like to PUT THE OIL ON THE STEAK, not pour it all over the flat grillplate, because all you get is the flavour of a lot of burnt oil. If you pour oil all over the chargrill, you simply need your head examined.
- You need the HOTPLATE HOT when the steaks go on or they'll stick to it and they won't caramelise properly.
- There are differing views on SEASONING. Some people think that salt before cooking draws the moisture out of a steak. I'm of the 'a little before on both sides and plenty at the table' school, but that's just a personal preference.
- THE MOST IMPORTANT THING, without doubt, is that you TURN THE BLOODY STEAKS ONCE ONLY. You want the natural sugars in the meat to caramelise and turn into a lovely brown crust. If you turn the steak, five, 10, 20 times and your mate turns it some more while you grab a beer, the steak will finish up like a piece of shoe leather. It is a mystery why the Australian male believes it is his mission on earth, to justify his position as holder of the tongs, to be constantly turning the steaks.

- If you give the steak A LITTLE REST after it's cooked, all the juices relax back into the fibres of the meat. Try taking a piece of steak direct from the grill and cutting it immediately; your plate will be covered in juices and blood. Rest the meat loosely covered with foil or a clean tea towel; don't seal tightly or the meat will keep cooking in the steam created. I prefer a clean tea towel, which keeps most of the heat in but allows for some air. Don't forget to spoon the delicious juices that have come from the meat back over them – you can't make a sauce that good.
- Don't put the cooked meat on the plate that it came to the barbecue on, with the blood still on it. Put it in a large bowl or on a CLEAN PLATE. Whenever I say this at cooking classes, there's always the 'Why do you have to do that, mate?' responses from the crowd. The obvious answer is 'So you don't poison everybody'.
- Like I said, it's only common sense.

THE PERFECT SAUSAGE
Similar thinking with the bangers.

- Some people think you need to boil them so they'll cook without exploding. I think you just need to cook them properly.
- Bring them back to ROOM TEMPERATURE, as with the steaks. Cook them on the FLAT GRILLPLATE not the chargrill. Some juices and fat are bound to escape and, if they're on the chargrill, it will ignite and cause flames that make for black, incinerated bangers.
- DON'T POKE THE BANGERS. They put everything inside the sausages for a reason. Poking them just lets a lot of those things, like moisture and flavour, escape. If you poke the bangers and put them on the chargrill, you also need your head examined, because you are almost guaranteed to incinerate the sausages and end up with the alternative perfect Aussie banger: black on the outside and raw in the middle.
- Cook the bangers over LOW HEAT and TURN THEM OFTEN to prevent burning. The idea is to cook them through and not have them split open. Low heat and frequent turning will help.

So the next time you're having a barbie, just try these steps and see what a difference it makes.

Steak with horseradish cream and potato cake

PREP **15 mins**   COOK **7–10 mins**   REST **5 mins**

So how much water do you think you can squeeze out of potatoes? If you haven't done it before, don't take any bets – because there's lots. And if you haven't tried fresh horseradish before, you're in for a treat, with its very clean, hot flavours. I suggest that you just keep adding more horseradish and tasting it until you get to the right heat level for your palate.

4 sirloin or Scotch fillet cut steaks, each about 200–250 g
2 tablespoons olive oil
sea salt and freshly ground black pepper, to taste

POTATO CAKE
2 large desiree potatoes
1 teaspoon pouring salt
1 teaspoon thyme leaves
50 g butter
2 tablespoons olive oil

HORSERADISH CREAM
1 tablespoon freshly grated horseradish
300 g creme fraiche or light sour cream
1 teaspoon white-wine vinegar
sea salt and freshly ground black pepper

1 Bring the meat to room temperature by removing from the fridge half an hour before cooking.
2 To make the potato cake, peel and grate the potatoes, then sprinkle with salt and place in a clean tea towel. Roll the tea towel up lengthways and twist its ends in opposite directions over a sink, getting rid of as much moisture as possible – there will be quite a bit. Unroll the tea towel and place the grated potato in a small bowl and add thyme leaves, mixing well.
3 Melt half the butter with the olive oil in a heavy-based 15–18 cm wide non-stick frying pan. Add the potatoes and push the mixture down with a potato masher or the back of a spoon. Cook over low–medium heat for about 4–5 minutes until it becomes crispy round the edge and the bottom of the potatoes turns brown. Carefully turn the potato cake out onto a plate the same size as the frying pan. Melt the remaining butter and slide the potato cake back into the pan, uncooked side down. Cook for about 3–4 minutes until well browned and crisp and slide out onto a chopping board.
4 While the potato is cooking, make the horseradish cream by mixing all the ingredients together in a small bowl. Set aside until ready to serve.
5 Also while the potatoes are cooking, brush the steaks with a little oil and season well with salt and pepper, then cook on a preheated chargrill or flat grillplate over high heat until done to your liking, turning once. Rest steaks, loosely covered, for 5 minutes before serving.
6 Serve the steaks with a dollop of the cream and a wedge of potato cake.

Serves 4

Veal with orange butter and fennel and orange salad

PREP 20 mins   MARINATE 2–3 hrs   COOK 3 mins

You can use thin slices of veal (as in the photo opposite) or you can use a veal cutlet; the flavours will be the same, but the meal a bit more substantial. The veal and orange butter tend to the sweet side of savoury, which is why the salty sharp salad balances things nicely.

8 veal steaks, each about ⅔ cm thick

MARINADE
1 onion, thinly sliced
8 sprigs thyme
juice of 1 orange

ORANGE BUTTER
200 g butter, softened
1 tablespoon thyme leaves
1 tablespoon very finely grated orange zest
1 teaspoon red chilli, seeded and finely diced
sea salt and freshly ground black pepper to taste

FENNEL AND ORANGE SALAD
3 tablespoons olive oil
1 tablespoon white-wine vinegar
1 teaspoon Dijon mustard
1 tablespoon orange juice
sea salt and freshly ground black pepper
1 cup picked watercress sprigs
1 small fennel bulb, hard core removed, finely sliced
1 orange, peeled and cut into segments
1 small red onion, finely sliced
½ cup black olives

1 Combine the marinade ingredients in a shallow glass or ceramic bowl and add the veal, turning to coat thoroughly. Cover with plastic film and leave in the fridge to marinate for 2–3 hours.
2 Bring the meat to room temperature by removing from the fridge half an hour before cooking.
3 To make the orange butter, combine all ingredients in a food processor and blend until smooth, or mash together with the back of a fork in a bowl. Place a sheet of baking paper on your workbench, with the butter in the centre. Use your hands to shape butter into a cylinder, then roll and twist the ends of the paper to make a bon bon. Refrigerate until ready to use.
4 To make the salad, mix together the oil, vinegar, mustard, orange juice, salt and pepper in a large salad bowl. Toss through the other ingredients.
5 Scrape the onion from the veal and cook veal on a preheated chargrill over high heat for a minute on each side, or until done to your liking.
6 Transfer the veal to four plates and top with slices of the orange butter. Serve immediately with the fennel salad.

Serves 4

BEEF

75

Teriyaki fillet steaks

PREP 10 mins   MARINATE 2 hrs   COOK 5 mins   REST 2 mins

This one is a children's favourite at Japanese restaurants, especially when it has too much sugar. You can use thinly sliced beef and cook this as a stir-fry or use 1 cm thick pieces of fillet and pan-fry them. Let's keep the sugar level at reasonable so it isn't the dominant flavour.

**8–12 thick beef fillet steaks (about 1 kg in total),
each about 1 cm thick**
3 tablespoons neutral oil
**1 spring onion, white and pale-green parts only,
sliced diagonally**
1 clove garlic, crushed
2 cups bean sprouts
1 tablespoon light soy sauce

MARINADE
1½ tablespoons dark soy sauce
1½ tablespoons mirin
1 tablespoon sake
1½–2 cm piece ginger, peeled and grated
1 clove garlic, grated
1½ tablespoons brown sugar

1 Combine the marinade ingredients in a shallow glass or ceramic bowl and add the steaks, turning to coat thoroughly. Cover with plastic film and leave in the fridge to marinate for 2 hours.
2 Bring the meat to room temperature by removing from the fridge half an hour before cooking.
3 Heat 2 tablespoons of oil in a frying pan or on a preheated flat grillplate over high heat and quickly cook the steaks, turning once, pouring over any leftover marinade as they cook, making sure that the marinade boils. Rest for a couple of minutes.
4 Heat remaining oil in the wok, and cook the spring onion and garlic for 30 seconds, then add the bean sprouts and soy sauce and cook for 1 minute. Set aside.
5 Serve steaks with bean sprouts.

Serves 4

Herb and parmesan crumbed veal cutlet >

PREP 10 mins   COOK 8–10 mins

It's important to find real veal for this. Hint: it should be pink and not blood-red. It's also important not to have your flat grillplate flat out or you'll burn the breadcrumbs before the meat is near cooked.
Use panko breadcrumbs if you can. If not, use fresh white breadcrumbs – dry breadcrumbs would be my third choice.

**⅔ cup (100 g) plain flour, seasoned with
sea salt and black pepper**
**1 free-range or organic egg, beaten with
a teaspoon of cold water**
**2 cups (140 g) panko dried breadcrumbs or
fresh white breadcrumbs**
½ cup (40 g) freshly, finely grated parmesan cheese
1 teaspoon thyme leaves, finely chopped
1 teaspoon chives, very finely chopped
1 tablespoon flat-leaf parsley, very finely chopped
sea salt and freshly ground black pepper
**4 veal cutlets, pounded with a meat mallet to
a thickness of about 1 cm**
½ cup (125 ml) olive oil
lemon wedges, to serve

1 To crumb the cutlets, take three shallow bowls. In one, place the seasoned flour; in the next, the beaten egg; and in the third, the breadcrumbs, parmesan, thyme, chives, parsley, salt and pepper, well-combined.
2 Dip each cutlet in the flour, covering it completely, then in the egg wash. Finally, immerse in the crumb mixture, pressing down on each side. Transfer cutlets to a clean plate.
3 Preheat the flat grillplate to medium and pour on ¾ of the oil. Place the crumbed cutlets on the grillplate and cook until golden-brown, then turn and drizzle the remaining oil around them, cooking until the second side is also golden-brown.
4 Remove cutlets from grillplate and drain on a paper towel for a minute. Serve with the lemon wedges and another sprinkle of salt.

Serves 4

Honey balsamic veal cutlets and braised peas

PREP 10 mins   COOK 20 mins

Yep, this is getting a bit fancy pants for the barbie, but the flavours all work very nicely together. It's a good dish for a school night, maybe sorting the peas inside and knocking the cutlets off al fresco.

4 veal cutlets
2 tablespoons honey
⅓ cup (80 ml) balsamic vinegar
1 teaspoon fresh thyme leaves
2 tablespoons butter
2 tablespoons olive oil

BRAISED PEAS
2 tablespoons olive oil
1 clove garlic, finely sliced
1 onion, finely sliced
2–3 cups shelled fresh peas
1 cup (250 ml) chicken stock
½ teaspoon salt
½ teaspoon sugar
½ teaspoon fresh thyme leaves

1 Bring the meat to room temperature by removing from the fridge half an hour before cooking.
2 Place the honey and balsamic in a small saucepan and cook over medium heat until it has reduced by half. Stir in the thyme leaves and butter and set aside.
3 To cook the peas, heat the oil in a saucepan or wok over medium heat, add the garlic and onion and soften without browning. Add the rest of the ingredients and bring to the boil, then simmer uncovered over low heat for about 10 minutes, until the liquid reduces and the peas are cooked.
4 While the peas are cooking, brush the veal with the olive oil and cook on preheated chargrill or flat grillplate over medium–high heat for about 3–4 minutes, or until done to your liking. When one side is nearly done, brush the top side with plenty of the glaze and turn over. Brush the other side well and turn again to cook for just a few seconds.
5 Serve immediately with a generous helping of braised peas.

Serves 4

Calf's liver and bacon with caramelised onions >

PREP 5 mins   COOK 20–25 mins

My dad used to eat lamb's liver in a humble cafe in Lismore in the '40s. Back then it was called lamb's fry. The onions would most certainly have been called fried, not caramelised as is the modern fashion, and people would think you were speaking Martian if you mentioned balsamic. The other certainty is that the liver would have been cooked to within an inch of its life. This isn't. Other than that, it's pretty much the same dish, using calf's liver.

120 ml olive oil
2 onions, thinly sliced
2 tablespoons balsamic vinegar
1 teaspoon brown sugar
4 slices calf's liver, each about 150–200 g
4 rashers rindless bacon
lemon wedges, to serve (optional)

1 Heat 4 tablespoons of oil in a wok or saucepan over medium–high heat and add the onions, cooking slowly and stirring frequently so that they colour without going crisp. As they start to colour, stir through the balsamic. The onions will reduce as the liquid in them evaporates. Add the occasional tablespoon of water to help them brown (we used to use beer back at the football club). When they are nicely reduced and caramelised, after about 10–15 minutes, add the brown sugar and simmer for a couple more minutes.
2 When the onions are nearly done, cook the bacon on a preheated flat grillplate over high heat until it begins to crisp. Sprinkle the remaining olive oil beside it and cook the calf's liver over very high heat for about 2 minutes on each side, or until done to your liking, turning once, until it is medium–rare.
3 Serve the liver topped with a rasher of bacon, lemon wedges and a spoonful of onions on top.

Serves 4

Sirloin with salsa verde butter and mushroom stack

PREP **15 mins**   COOK **10–15 mins**   REST **5 mins**

This is a bit of fun on your chums' plates at a barbecue, and very easy to pull off. You make the flavoured butter well ahead of time and can freeze any leftover for your next barbecue.

4 sirloin steaks, each about 250 g and 3 cm thick, trimmed of excess fat
⅓ cup (80 ml) olive oil
sea salt and freshly ground black pepper, to taste
1 clove garlic, crushed or chopped
4 each of field, portobello, pine, oyster and shiitake mushrooms, as close to the same size as possible
green salad, to serve

SALSA VERDE BUTTER
1 large clove garlic, finely chopped or crushed
1 teaspoon salted capers, rinsed and finely chopped
handful of basil, roughly chopped
handful of flat-leaf parsley, roughly chopped
250 g butter, cut into 2 cm cubes
1 teaspoon lemon juice
sea salt and freshly ground black pepper

1 Bring the meat to room temperature by removing from the fridge half an hour before cooking.
2 To make the salsa verde butter, place the garlic, capers, basil and parsley in a food processor and pulse until the herbs are finely chopped. Add butter and lemon juice and a little salt and pepper and pulse some more, until the herbs are mixed completely through the butter.
3 Place a sheet of baking paper on your workbench, with the butter in the centre. Use your hands to shape butter into a cylinder, then roll and twist the ends of the paper to make a bon bon. Refrigerate until ready to use.
4 Brush each steak with about a tablespoon of oil and season both sides with salt and pepper, then cook on a preheated chargrill or flat grillplate over high heat for about 4–5 minutes on each side, or until done to your liking, turning once.
5 While the steaks are cooking, mix the garlic with the rest of the olive oil in a small bowl and brush or spoon over the mushrooms. Cook the mushrooms with the steak for about 4–5 minutes each side until just cooked, but still slightly firm.
6 Rest steaks, loosely covered, for 5 minutes before serving.
7 Place a disc of the butter on top of each steak, stack the different mushrooms on top of each other beside the steak and serve immediately with a little green salad.

Serves 4

BEEF

Sirloin steaks with maitre d'hotel butter

PREP 10 mins　COOK 6–8 mins　REST 5 mins

You can busy this butter up with garlic, shallots, thyme, whatever else, but a proper maitre d'hotel butter should be blissfully simple: butter, parsley and lemon juice; salt and pepper if pushed.

Keep it simple and enjoy it on any steak you like.

4 sirloin steaks, each about 250–300 g
2 tablespoons olive oil
sea salt and freshly ground black pepper

MAITRE D'HOTEL BUTTER
2 tablespoons flat-leaf parsley, finely chopped
2 tablespoons lemon juice
pinch sea salt
½ teaspoon freshly ground black pepper
150 g butter, cut into 1 cm cubes

1 Bring the meat to room temperature by removing from the fridge half an hour before cooking.
2 To make the maitre d'hotel butter, in a small bowl mash the parsley, lemon juice, salt and pepper with the back of a fork into the butter. Place a sheet of baking paper on your workbench, and put the butter in the centre. Use your hands to shape butter into a cylinder, then roll and twist the ends of the paper to make a bon bon. Refrigerate until ready to use.
3 Brush the steaks with a little oil and season with salt and pepper, then cook on a preheated chargrill or flat grillplate over high heat for 3–4 minutes on each side, turning once, or until done to your liking. Rest steaks, loosely covered, for 5 minutes before serving.
4 Serve with a disc of butter on top, and drizzle over any juices from the resting.

Serves 4

Black pepper and mustard filet mignon >

PREP 10 mins　COOK 10 mins　REST 5 mins

Here the old 'black pepper steak' from bad steak houses of my youth meets filet mignon.

I have not-so-happy memories of tough, greasy, acrid peppery steaks back then. This is the opposite; miles of flavour and clean as a whistle.

4 pieces beef fillet, preferably centre-cut, each about
**　250 g and about 6 cm thick, trimmed of excess fat**
⅓ cup (95 g) Dijon mustard
⅓ cup (50 g) freshly ground black pepper
2 teaspoons sea salt
2 tablespoons olive oil
mashed or boiled potatoes and green salad,
**　to serve (optional)**

1 Bring the meat to room temperature by removing from the fridge half an hour before cooking.
2 Spread one tablespoon of mustard all the way around the edge of each steak. Place a piece of baking paper on your workbench and on it mix together a tablespoon of pepper and half a teaspoon of salt. Roll each steak along its mustard-coated edge in the pepper and salt, coating edge evenly.
3 Brush the flat top of each steak with oil and season with a little more salt if you like. Cook, oiled-side down, on a preheated flat grillplate over medium–high heat (it's a thick steak and needs to cook through) for about 5 minutes on each side, or until done to your liking. Brush the other flat side with oil and season again before turning, then cook to desired done-ness. Rest, loosely covered, for 5 minutes before serving, spooning over any yummy juices from the resting process.
4 Serve with potatoes and a nice, sharply dressed green salad if you like, or the Spicy Potato Bake (pictured) on page 174.

Serves 4

World's fastest steak marinade

PREP **5 mins**   MARINATE **2–4 hrs**   COOK **8–10 mins**   REST **5 mins**

Nothing too cerebral here.

Take a mortar and pestle and about 2 minutes of your life and you're done.

Ideally, you would let the steaks marinate covered in the fridge for a few hours, but if you're pressed for time, throw them straight on the barbie, and the flavours will still come through. You can use this on whatever type of steak you like.

4 steaks, preferably sirloin

MARINADE
1 teaspoon fennel seeds
2 tablespoons olive oil
2 cloves garlic, crushed
zest of one lemon, very finely grated
1 teaspoon freshly ground black pepper
1 teaspoon ground oregano
½ teaspoon ground cumin
½ teaspoon celery salt
pinch of cayenne pepper

1 To make the marinade, simply pound the fennel seeds in a mortar and pestle until broken up (or you can try chopping them with a knife, but they'll jump everywhere) and combine with all the other ingredients in a small bowl, mixing well.
2 Place the steaks in a shallow glass or ceramic bowl and coat with the marinade, then cover with plastic film and marinate in the fridge for 2–4 hours.
3 Bring the steaks to room temperature by removing from the fridge half an hour before cooking, and cook on a preheated chargrill over high heat for about 4–5 minutes each side, or until done to your liking, turning once. Rest steaks, loosely covered, for 5 minutes before serving.

Serves 4

T-Bone with herb aioli >

PREP **10 mins**   COOK **8–12 mins**   REST **5 mins**

There's something nice and simple about this. You could have a thicker steak and just squeeze lemon on it and call it Bistecca Florentina, but a simple well-cooked steak, especially a T-bone with a big dollop of garlicky, herby mayo, is pretty much to die for – though cook it every night and you just might.

4 pieces T-bone, each about 300–400g
2 tablespoons olive oil
sea salt and freshly ground pepper, to taste
green salad, to serve

HERB AIOLI
4 cloves garlic, crushed or chopped
4 free-range or organic egg yolks
1 teaspoon Dijon mustard
1 tablespoon basil leaves, finely chopped
1 tablespoon oregano or marjoram leaves, finely chopped
1 tablespoon flat-leaf parsley leaves, finely chopped
150 ml extra virgin olive oil
100 ml neutral oil
1 tablespoon lemon juice
sea salt, to taste

1 Bring the meat to room temperature by removing from the fridge half an hour before cooking.
2 To make the aioli, place the garlic, egg yolks and mustard in a food processor and mix well. Add the herbs, mixing well, then add the oils in the thinnest possible stream, and continue to blend until the mixture is thick. Add the lemon juice and taste, adding more lemon or some salt if necessary. Pour into a small jug or bowl and refrigerate, covered, until ready to use.
3 Brush the steaks with a little oil and season well with salt and pepper, then cook on a preheated chargrill over medium–high heat for about 4–6 minutes on each side, or until done to your liking, turning once. Rest steaks, loosely covered, for 5 minutes before serving.
4 Serve with a nice dollop of aioli and salads or vegies of your choice, like the Roast Balsamic Red Onions and Treviso with Thyme (pictured) on page 171.

Serves 4

< Beef kebabs with chimichurri sauce

PREP 15 mins   COOK 6–8 mins   REST 5 mins

For some reason a lot of people think that chimichurri is some sort of chilli sauce, but it's actually more like a South American pesto, with lots of garlic, herbs and oil.

Enjoy it with these kebabs or really any steak at all.

600–800 g lean rump steak, cut into 2 cm cubes
1 red onion, chopped into 2 cm dice
sea salt and freshly ground black pepper
2 tablespoons olive oil

CHIMICHURRI SAUCE
1 large handful flat-leaf parsley, chopped
8 cloves garlic, peeled and chopped
1 teaspoon dried oregano leaves or 1 tablespoon
  fresh oregano, chopped
1 cup (250 ml) olive oil
¼ cup (60 ml) red-wine vinegar
2 tablespoons lemon juice
1 teaspoon sea salt
½ teaspoon black pepper
½ teaspoon chilli flakes (optional)

1 Bring the meat to room temperature by removing from the fridge half an hour before cooking.
2 To make the chimichurri sauce, place all ingredients in a food processor or blender and pulse until combined. Set aside.
3 Thread the steak cubes and onion dice onto skewers, brush with a little oil then season well with salt and pepper. Cook the skewers on a preheated chargrill or flat grillplate over high heat for 3–4 minutes each side, or until done to your liking, turning once.
4 Remove the skewers and set them aside to rest, loosely covered, for 5 minutes before serving.
5 Serve with a generous dollop of chimichurri sauce on top.

Serves 4

Rump steak with old-fashioned mushroom sauce

PREP 5 mins   COOK 10–15 mins   REST 5 mins

This is one of my favourite public bar dishes at the Four in Hand or the Grand National, happily just blocks from my home in Paddington. In ancient times, this would have been a counter lunch; it's nice to have something this plain instead of a tricked-up dish in a flash pub restaurant.

I don't use cream, as it dilutes the flavours too much, and I prefer the stronger-flavoured portobello mushrooms to the milder buttons or even field mushrooms.

1 piece of good-quality rump steak, approximately
  450–500 g, halved crossways
1 tablespoon olive oil
sea salt and freshly ground black pepper

MUSHROOM SAUCE
4 medium portobello mushrooms
25 g butter
1 tablespoon olive oil
1 clove garlic, crushed
250 ml good-quality beef stock
½–1 teaspoon fresh thyme leaves
sea salt and freshly ground black pepper

1 Bring the meat to room temperature by removing from the fridge half an hour before cooking.
2 Brush the steak with a little olive oil and season with salt and pepper. Cook on a preheated chargrill or flat grillplate over high heat, for about 3–4 minutes each side, or until done to your liking, turning once. Rest steaks, loosely covered, for 5 minutes.
3 While the steak is cooking, make the sauce. Cut the mushrooms in half crossways, then slice them. Melt the butter and oil in a frying pan over medium heat, add the mushrooms and fry until they begin to brown and soften. Add the garlic, stock and thyme leaves and season with
salt and pepper to taste – you probably won't need much salt, but it depends on how salty the stock is. Simmer for about 5–10 minutes until the sauce has reduced and thickened slightly.
4 Serve the steaks with a generous amount of sauce spooned over the top.

Serves 2

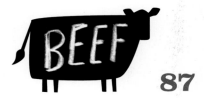

Filet mignon with red wine sauce

PREP 10 mins   COOK 20–25 mins   REST 5 mins

You could say this is pretty pretentious barbecue fare, but it's surprisingly easy to do and makes a very nice winter lunch or dinner. I'd make the effort to cook some spuds and green vegetables rather than pair this with barbecue salads.

Make sure that you use a reasonable bottle of red for the sauce. No one is suggesting your oldest vintage of Grange, but don't use rubbish or the sauce will taste of it.

4 pieces thick beef fillet, preferably centre-cut, trimmed of excess fat
4 thin slices rindless bacon or prosciutto (I prefer the latter)
sea salt and freshly ground black pepper
2 tablespoons olive oil
vegetables, to serve

RED WINE SAUCE
3 cups (750 ml) red wine
2 bay leaves
½ small onion or a golden shallot, chopped
½ carrot, chopped
¼ stick celery, thinly sliced
3 or 4 parsley stalks
approximately 6 whole black peppercorns
50 g butter

1 Bring the meat to room temperature by removing from the fridge half an hour before cooking.
2 To make the sauce, place all ingredients except the butter in a saucepan and bring to the boil, then reduce heat for 20 minutes, or until only about ½–⅔ cup of liquid remains. Strain through a sieve and return to the rinsed-out saucepan, reducing a little more. Remove the sauce from the heat and whisk through the butter. Pour into a small jug and set aside.
3 While the sauce is reducing, wrap a piece of bacon or prosciutto around each steak and secure with a toothpick if necessary. Season with salt and pepper and rub each end of the steaks with oil, then cook on a preheated chargrill or flat grillplate over medium–high heat, for about 5 minutes, or until done to your liking, turning once until done.
4 Rest steaks, loosely covered, for 5 minutes before serving.
5 Serve the steaks with vegetables on warm plates, pouring the sauce over the top at the table.

Serves 4

BEEF

'Back to front' marinated steak

PREP 5 mins   MARINATE 7 mins   COOK 10–15 mins

Most meat is marinated in dry spices (a dry rub) or a traditional wet marinade which may include spices, garlic, wine, whatever.

This recipe marinates the meat after it is cooked so it takes no extra time at all. Italians have long used a bagna cauda, or warm bath of garlic, oil, fresh herbs and sometimes anchovies, to flavour vegetables after they're cooked, and this is exactly the same principle. If you prefer, two very thick sirloin steaks will work just as well.

800 g–1 kg piece of rump steak in a single piece
   (it should be 2–4 cm thick)
2 tablespoons olive oil
sea salt and freshly ground black pepper
2 bunches asparagus, woody ends removed
boiled potatoes, to serve

MARINADE
¾ cup (180 ml) olive oil
2 cloves garlic, crushed
2 anchovies, finely chopped
2 tablespoons rosemary leaves, finely chopped
juice and finely grated zest of half a lemon
sea salt and freshly ground black pepper

1 Bring the meat to room temperature by removing from the fridge half an hour before cooking.
2 Brush both sides of the steak with a little oil and season well with salt and pepper. Cook the steak on a preheated chargrill over medium heat (it's a thick lump of meat and you don't want it black as charcoal) for about 5–7 minutes on each side if you like it medium–rare, or until done to your liking. When you turn the meat, place the asparagus on the chargrill and cook for a couple of minutes until they begin to colour and soften.
3 When the meat is nearly done, make the marinade by placing a tablespoon of oil in a small baking dish on the barbecue. Add the garlic and anchovies and stir over medium heat for about 2 minutes until the anchovies 'melt' and the garlic is a pale golden-brown. Add the rosemary and the rest of the oil until it is just warmed through. Add the lemon juice and zest and plenty of salt and pepper.
4 Place the steak and asparagus in the baking dish with the marinade and cover loosely. Turn the steak after 5 minutes, then leave to marinate for another 2 minutes. Remove the steak and cut into thick slices.
5 Serve with the asparagus, potatoes and the remaining marinade spooned over the top.

Serves 4

East-West lamb

PREP 10 mins MARINATE 4–12 hrs COOK 20–30 mins REST 10 mins

It doesn't seem to make much sense, putting soy sauce and ginger with mustard and Worcestershire, but all that matters is that it works.

1 boned leg of lamb, 1.2–1.4 kg, trimmed of excess fat and butterflied (ask your butcher to do this for you)
3–4 cm piece ginger, peeled and thinly sliced
6 cloves garlic
zest and juice of 1 lemon
2 tablespoons soy sauce
2 tablespoons brown sugar
2 tablespoons Worcestershire sauce
1 tablespoon dry mustard
1 tablespoon sea salt
2 tablespoons Dijon mustard
⅓ cup (80 ml) neutral oil
Chinese green vegetables, to serve

1 Combine all ingredients except lamb and vegetables in a food processor and blend to a smooth paste. Place lamb in a large shallow dish and coat both sides with the paste. Cover with plastic film and marinate in the fridge for 4–12 hours. Bring the meat to room temperature by removing from the fridge half an hour before cooking.
2 Cook lamb on a preheated lightly oiled flat grillplate over medium–high heat for about 10–15 minutes on each side, or until done to your liking, basting with any remaining marinade until the last 5 minutes of cooking.
3 Remove lamb from barbecue and rest on a plate, loosely covered, for 10 minutes before serving. Serve with steamed Chinese green vegetables.

Serves 6–8

Double-cut lamb chops with apple chutney >

PREP 15 mins COOK 30 mins REST 5 mins

This is the meat lovers' way to eat lamb – lots of it. You might need a bit of practice to get a feel for the done-ness of meat this thick on the bone, but the trick is not to have the barbie screaming hot. Note, this is not a cut for people who like well-done meat.

8 short loin lamb chops cut 5–6 cm thick
sea salt and freshly ground black pepper, to taste
1 tablespoon neutral oil
mashed potatoes, to serve (optional)

APPLE CHUTNEY
1 small red onion, cut into 1 cm pieces
1 red chilli, seeded and very finely diced
1 tablespoon of neutral oil
2 granny smith apples, peeled, cored and cut into dice of about 1 cm
100 g sultanas
1 heaped teaspoon ground cinnamon
¼ teaspoon allspice
¼ teaspoon ground nutmeg
2 tablespoons brown sugar
2 tablespoons cider vinegar
about 2 tablespoons water

1 To make the chutney, cook the onion and chilli in the oil in a saucepan over low heat for about 5 minutes without letting them colour. Add the apples and sultanas and cook them over medium heat for about 5 minutes, stirring regularly until the apple has softened. Stir through the cinnamon, allspice, nutmeg and brown sugar, and cook until the sugar has dissolved. Add the vinegar and enough water so that all of the ingredients are just covered. Simmer over low heat for about 20 minutes, until the apples have broken down and the mixture has become a bit jammy. Set aside.
2 Bring the lamb chops to room temperature by removing them from the fridge half an hour before cooking. Season well with salt and pepper and roll the 'tails' around the rest of the chops and tie with string, to prevent the 'tails' from escaping.
3 Cook on a preheated flat grillplate over medium heat until the meat colours one-third of the way up, or until done to your liking, then turn. Remove from the barbecue and set aside to rest, loosely covered, for about 5 minutes.
4 Serve two per person with a big dollop of warm chutney and maybe some mashed potatoes.

Serves 4 heartily

Kashmiri-spiced lamb cutlets with mustard potatoes and spicy salad

PREP **15 mins**   MARINATE **4–12 hrs**   COOK **20–25 mins**   REST **5 mins**

This is an easy-as way to capture some yummy and authentic Indian flavours on your barbecue. The lamb, potatoes and salad work very nicely together. Kashmiri chilli powder is a medium–hot chilli powder which is bright red in colour, and is available from specialty food stores. If you can't find it, use ordinary chilli powder.

12–16 lamb cutlets, not too trimmed

MARINADE
1 teaspoon Kashmiri chilli powder, more to taste
1 teaspoon sweet paprika
1 tablespoon ground coriander
1 tablespoon ground cumin
2 tablespoons neutral oil

MUSTARD POTATOES
2 large waxy potatoes, peeled
2 tablespoons neutral oil
1 tablespoon black mustard seeds
1 teaspoon ground turmeric
1 teaspoon ground coriander
½ teaspoon cumin seeds
20 curry leaves
1 onion, finely sliced
1½–2 cm piece ginger, peeled and grated
1 green chilli, seeded (unless you want it extra hot)
   and finely sliced
1 pinch salt

SPICY SALAD
2 tomatoes, sliced
1 Lebanese cucumber, sliced
1 red onion, sliced
2 tablespoons neutral oil
2 tablespoons lemon juice
½ green chilli, seeded and finely sliced
¼ teaspoon Kashmiri chilli powder
⅓ teaspoon ground cumin
1 pinch salt

1 Combine the marinade ingredients in a shallow glass or ceramic bowl and add the lamb cutlets, turning to coat thoroughly. Cover with plastic film and leave in the fridge to marinate for 4–12 hours. Bring the meat to room temperature by removing from the fridge half an hour before cooking.

2 To cook the potatoes, chop them into 2–3 cm dice, then heat the oil in a wok or deep frying pan over high heat and add mustard seeds. When they pop, add the dry spices, curry leaves, onion, ginger, chilli and salt, cooking for about 2–3 minutes until the onion softens. Add the potatoes and just enough water to cover them. Bring to the boil then simmer for about 10–15 minutes, stirring occasionally until the water is absorbed and the potatoes are cooked.

3 Cook the cutlets on a preheated flat grillplate over high heat for about 3–4 minutes each side until they are medium to medium–rare, or until done to your liking.

4 While the lamb is cooking, assemble the salad on a large serving plate, starting with a layer of tomato, then cucumber, then onion. Drizzle oil and lemon juice over the top, then sprinkle with chilli pieces, chilli powder, cumin and a big pinch of salt.

5 When the lamb cutlets are cooked, remove from the grill and set aside to rest, loosely covered, for about 5 minutes.

6 Serve three or four cutlets on each plate, pouring over any juices from the resting meat.

Serves 4

Ras el hanout lamb bruschetta with yoghurt dressing

PREP 10 mins   MARINATE 2–4 hrs   COOK 10–15 mins   REST 5 mins

This is a great barbecue lunch and a nice alternative to a quarter-kilo lump of meat.

Because of the size of the loins, or backstraps as they are sometimes called, they don't need to marinate for long. Lots of delicious big flavours here.

3 lamb loins or backstraps, stripped of all fat and sinew
¼ cup (60 ml) olive oil
2 tablespoons ras el hanout spice blend
2 red capsicums, white insides and seeds removed,
  cut into 2 cm strips
1 teaspoon white-wine vinegar
1 handful baby rocket leaves
4 thick slices rustic Italian bread, such as ciabatta
1 clove garlic, cut in half
freshly ground black pepper

YOGHURT DRESSING
1 tablespoon olive oil
1 cup (280 g) plain or Greek-style yoghurt
2 tablespoons lemon juice
½ teaspoon ground cumin
sea salt and freshly ground black pepper

1 Brush both sides of the lamb with 2 tablespoons of the oil and sprinkle with ras el hanout. Cover with plastic film and leave to marinate in the fridge for 2–4 hours.
2 Bring the meat to room temperature by removing from the fridge half an hour before cooking.
3 To make the dressing, mix together the olive oil, yoghurt, lemon juice, cumin, and a little salt and plenty of pepper in a small bowl. Set aside.
4 Cook the capsicum over high heat on a lightly oiled chargrill for about 5–6 minutes. Add the lamb and cook for about 2 minutes each side, until the lamb is medium–rare, or until done to your liking. Once cooked, remove the lamb from the grill and rest, loosely covered, for about 5 minutes while you chargrill the bread for about 1–2 minutes on each side. Set capsicum aside.
5 Mix the rest of the oil with the vinegar in a salad bowl, and toss through the rocket leaves.
6 Rub each slice of bread with the cut garlic, and place bread on four plates. Top the bread with the dressed rocket leaves, then the capsicum. Slice the lamb on the diagonal and pile slices on top of the capsicum.
7 Drizzle the yoghurt dressing over the top and finish with a good grinding of pepper.

Serves 4

Warm dukkah-crusted lamb salad

PREP **30 mins**   COOK **15–20 mins**   REST **5 mins**

This is one of my favourite dishes in this book. Recipes evolve for me and this is a twist on the Chicken and Bread Salad recipe from my book, *The Great Aussie Family Cookbook*, which came from a fantastic meal that I had at the fabulous Zuni Café in San Francisco more than a decade ago. I suggest that you have a crack at this for lunch one Sunday soon.

3–4 lamb loins or backstraps, stripped of all fat and sinew
½ cup (80 g) currants
1 tablespoon white-wine vinegar
2 tablespoons pine nuts
200 g (3–4 thick slices) day-old rustic bread (not sourdough), crust removed, torn into 3–4 cm pieces
⅓ cup (80 ml) olive oil
2 leeks, white and pale green parts only, sliced
1 small butter lettuce, washed and dried, tough outer leaves discarded
250 g cherry tomatoes
about 20 mint leaves, torn

DRESSING
120 ml olive oil
2 tablespoons white-wine vinegar
sea salt and freshly ground black pepper

DUKKAH MIX
2 tablespoons cumin seeds
2 tablespoons ground coriander
2 tablespoons sesame seeds
½ cup (70 g) blanched or slivered almonds
½ cup (75 g) shelled, unsalted pistachio nuts
1 teaspoon sea salt

1 Bring the meat to room temperature by removing from the fridge half an hour before cooking.
2 Soak the currants in vinegar for half an hour. Drain and set aside.
3 Lightly toast the pine nuts in a dry non-stick frying pan over high heat for a couple of minutes, watching closely so they don't burn, until they are golden-brown. Set aside.
4 Place the bread on a baking tray and cook in a very hot (220°C) oven for about 10 minutes, keeping an eye on it, until it is golden-brown. (You could do this in the barbecue with the lid down, but the oven is quicker). Set aside.
5 To make the dressing, mix together olive oil, vinegar, salt and pepper in a small jug.
6 To make the dukkah mix, place all dukkah ingredients in a food processor and blend to a coarse consistency. Transfer to a shallow bowl or plate. Coat the lamb with 3 tablespoons of oil and press both sides down into the dukkah mix until lamb is well-covered.
7 Add the rest of the oil to the pan and cook the leeks over medium heat until they soften. Allow to cool.
8 Fry lamb on a lightly oiled flat grillplate over medium–high heat for about 3–4 minutes each side until medium–rare, or until done to your liking. Rest, loosely covered, for about 5 minutes.
9 Arrange the bread and lettuce on a large serving platter and cover with tomatoes, leeks, currants and mint. Thinly slice the lamb and arrange on top then pour the dressing over the top. Sprinkle with pine nuts and serve.

Serves 4 comfortably

LAMB

Black pepper and maple lamb cutlets

PREP **10 mins** MARINATE **30 mins** COOK **5 mins** REST **5 mins**

The combination of lamb cutlets (heaven on a stick) with the sweetness of maple syrup will have these disappearing like hot cakes.

You need to be careful barbecuing anything with a high sugar content like maple syrup or sweet commercial marinades, because the sugar will burn – see below.

16 lamb cutlets, trimmed of excess fat
1 butter lettuce
12 cherry tomatoes, halved
1 red onion, very finely sliced
2 tablespoons olive oil
sea salt, to taste

MARINADE
½ cup (125 ml) maple syrup (real, not flavoured)
2 tablespoons coarsely ground black pepper
1 tablespoon rosemary leaves, very finely chopped
1 tablespoon olive oil

1 Combine the marinade ingredients in a shallow glass or ceramic bowl and add the lamb cutlets, turning to coat thoroughly. Cover with plastic film and leave to marinate in a cool place (not the fridge) for half an hour.
2 Cook cutlets on a preheated chargrill over medium–high heat for about 2 minutes on each side, turning a few times so the maple syrup doesn't burn and blacken, until the lamb is medium–rare, or until done to your liking. Remove the cutlets to a bowl and rest, loosely covered, for about 5 minutes before serving.
3 Arrange the lettuce on a large serving platter and scatter the tomatoes and onion over the top. Drizzle the oil over the salad and put the lamb cutlets on top, spooning over any remaining juices from the resting process and adding a generous sprinkle of salt.

Serves 4

Chermoula-crusted leg of lamb >

PREP **10 mins** MARINATE **2–4hrs** COOK **25–30 mins** REST **10 mins**

A good chermoula paste is nice and easy to whip up in a food processor.

Here I've whacked it on a butterflied leg of lamb, but it works on virtually all lamb cuts, it's terrific on chicken and works with fish and shellfish too.

A chermoula-crusted lamb leg isn't the prettiest dish you'll ever see, but the flavours are big and bold and work fantastically on the barbie.

1 large boned leg of lamb, about 1.2–1.4 kg, trimmed of excess fat and butterflied (ask your butcher to do this for you)
1 small handful coriander leaves
2 cloves garlic, crushed
1 small red onion, chopped
1½–2 cm piece ginger, peeled and chopped
2 red bird's-eye chillies, seeded and chopped
1 tablespoon sweet paprika
2 tablespoons ground cumin
2 tablespoons ground coriander
½ cup lemon juice
⅓ cup (80 ml) olive oil
1 teaspoon sea salt
lemon wedges, to serve (optional)

1 Combine all ingredients except lamb in a food processor and blend to a smooth paste. Place lamb in a shallow dish and coat with the paste, then cover with plastic film and marinate in the fridge for 2–4 hours. Bring the meat to room temperature by removing from the fridge half an hour before cooking.
2 Cook on a preheated lightly oiled flat grillplate over high heat for about 15 minutes each side, or until done to your liking.
3 Remove the lamb and set aside to rest, loosely covered, for 10 minutes, then carve into thick slices, serving with lemon segments and maybe some Tabbouleh (pictured), see page 164.

Serves 6–8

Oregano lamb cutlets with Greek salad

PREP 15 mins   MARINATE 2–4 hrs   COOK 5 mins   REST 5 mins

What could be a more Greek combination than lamb with oregano and a traditional Greek salad?

All very simple and basic but the flavours really work.

12 lamb cutlets 'restaurant cut' and trimmed of fat (ask your butcher to do this for you) or with extra fat and meat left on
lemon wedges, to serve

MARINADE
2 tablespoons dried oregano leaves
1 teaspoon sea salt
½ teaspoon freshly ground black pepper
finely grated zest of half a lemon
3 cloves garlic, crushed or grated
½ cup (125 ml) olive oil

GREEK SALAD
2 tomatoes
1 large Lebanese cucumber, peeled or partially peeled, seeded if you like, and cut into 2–3 cm pieces
3 tablespoons olive oil
2 tablespoons white vinegar
sea salt and black pepper to taste
1 green capsicum, white insides and seeds removed, sliced
½ iceberg lettuce, cut into wedges
½ red onion, thinly sliced
16 pitted kalamata olives
150 g feta cheese (preferably Greek), cut into 2 cm cubes
½ teaspoon dried oregano leaves

1 Combine the marinade ingredients in a shallow glass or ceramic bowl and add the lamb cutlets, turning to coat thoroughly. Cover with plastic film and leave in the fridge to marinate for 2–4 hours.
2 Bring the meat back to room temperature by removing from the fridge half an hour before cooking.
3 Cook cutlets on a preheated chargrill over high heat for a couple of minutes on each side, or until done to your liking. Once cooked, remove from grill and rest, loosely covered, for about 5 minutes.
4 To make the salad, cut tomatoes and cucumber into even pieces (about 2–3 cm). Mix together the oil, vinegar, salt and pepper in a large salad bowl and toss through the tomatoes, cucumber, capsicum, lettuce, onion, olives and cheese, mixing well, then sprinkle over the oregano.
5 Place the shredded iceberg lettuce on a large serving platter (to soak up the yummy juices) and arrange the cutlets on top, pouring over any juices from the resting process.
6 Serve with lemon wedges and salad.

Serves 4

Lamb chops with chargrilled ratatouille

PREP 15 mins   COOK 6–8 mins   REST 5 mins

Ratatouille is one of those simple dishes that a lot of restaurants mess up, serving a sludge of vegetables, often drowning in tomato paste. In a good one, the vegetables are cooked separately, so they retain their own flavour, then combined.

Here we're borrowing the name, taking most of the ingredients but completely changing the cooking method by chargrilling the vegetables, which go very nicely with some lamb chops.

8 lamb short loin chops
1 tablespoon olive oil
sea salt and freshly ground black pepper, to taste
⅔ cup (160 ml) garlic-flavoured olive oil or olive oil
  with 4 crushed cloves garlic in it
1 large onion, cut into 4 slices, 1½ cm thick
1 eggplant, cut into 4 slices, 1½ cm thick
2 large red capsicum, white insides and seeds removed,
  cored and halved lengthways, trimmed to be mostly flat
2 large tomatoes, cut into 4 slices, 1½ cm thick
4 zucchini, each cut into 2–3 slices lengthways
8 basil leaves, shredded

1 Bring the lamb chops to room temperature by removing from the fridge half an hour before cooking. Brush them with the oil and season with salt and pepper then cook on a preheated flat grillplate over medium–high heat for 3–4 minutes on each side, or until done to your liking.
2 Meanwhile, brush all the vegetables with the garlic oil and cook onion, eggplant and capsicum on a preheated chargrill over high heat for about 3 minutes. Add tomatoes and zucchini, and cook for a further 2 minutes.
3 Rest lamb chops, loosely covered, for about 5 minutes, then serve, drizzling over any juices from the resting and sprinkling with a little salt. Stack the vegetables on top of each other beside the lamb chops and top with the basil leaves, drizzling over any leftover garlic oil or some plain olive oil and a grinding of pepper.

Serves 4

Kebabs not like the fluoro takeaway shops >

PREP 15 mins   COOK 8–10 mins

Hands up who hasn't wound up in a greasy, over-lit kebab shop after a night on the tiles. It doesn't matter – I can't see your hand – and I've wound up in much worse places.

The point is that a kebab doesn't have to be greasy and disgusting. It can be a quick and delicious lunch and not even too bad for you either.

600 g lamb mince (not too lean)
1 clove garlic, grated
2 red onions, one grated, one very finely sliced
1 teaspoon dried oregano leaves
1 teaspoon salt
¼ cup (60 ml) olive oil
4 small pita bread rounds
large handful flat-leaf parsley, roughly chopped
1 tomato, thinly sliced
4 tablespoons Tzatziki Salad (see page 106)
juice of ½ lemon
2 teaspoons paprika (not smoked)
sea salt and freshly ground pepper (optional)

1 Combine the lamb, garlic, grated onion, oregano and salt in a large bowl and mix really well with your hands. Divide the mixture and shape along four solid metal skewers (aiming for the meat to be slightly smaller than the pita bread).
2 Brush the preheated flat grillplate with half the oil, and carefully cook the kebabs over very high heat for about 4–5 minutes on each side until nicely charred but moist in the middle (a dry kebab is a crook kebab!), or until done to your liking.
3 Brush the pita bread with the remaining oil and cook on the grillplate for a few seconds each side to warm them up.
4 Place each warm pita bread on a plate and place the parsley, sliced onion and tomato in a line about 3–4 cm in from one edge, then drizzle with the tzatziki. Remove the skewers from the kebabs (without burning or skewering yourself) and place lamb on top of the salad. Squeeze some lemon juice over the top of each and dust with paprika, adding salt and pepper if you like, though they mightn't need them.
5 Roll tightly and eat with the juices dripping into your lap. For authentic effect, forget that you ate them until reminded the next day.

Serves 4 with a beer you don't need

Cumin lamb fillets with tzatziki salad

PREP **15 mins**   MARINATE **2–4 hrs**   COOK **4 mins**   REST **5 mins**

You can cook this with lamb cutlets instead of fillets, and the tzatziki is a bit more substantial than the traditional recipe, which is really more of a dip. The chunky pieces of vegetable make it more of a match for the lamb.

8–12 lamb fillets
sea salt, to taste
lemon wedges, to serve

MARINADE
1 heaped tablespoon cumin seeds
⅔ cup (190 g) plain or Greek-style yoghurt
½ teaspoon chilli flakes
zest of 1 lemon, finely grated
4 cloves garlic, finely grated or crushed
½ cup (125 ml) olive oil
1 tablespoon sea salt
1 teaspoon freshly ground black pepper

TZATZIKI SALAD
250 g Greek-style yoghurt
3 Lebanese cucumbers, peeled and seeds removed
juice and finely grated zest of 1 lemon
2 cloves garlic, grated or crushed
½ teaspoon salt
½ teaspoon white pepper
2 tablespoons olive oil
1 witlof, core discarded, leaves washed and
    dried and cut in half, crossways
2 sticks celery, sliced

1 Combine the marinade ingredients in a shallow glass or ceramic bowl and add the lamb pieces, turning to coat thoroughly. Cover with plastic film and leave in the fridge to marinate for 2–4 hours.
2 Bring the meat to room temperature by removing from the fridge half an hour before cooking.
3 To make the salad, place the yoghurt in a salad bowl and coarsely grate one of the cucumbers into it. Add the lemon juice and zest, garlic, salt, pepper and olive oil and mix well to combine. Chop remaining cucumbers into 2 cm chunks and fold through, with the witlof leaves and celery. Refrigerate, covered, until ready to use.
4 Thread the lamb fillets onto skewers through the thickest end, and cook on a preheated chargrill or flat grillplate over high heat for about a minute or two on each side until medium–rare, or until done to your liking.
5 Remove the skewers from the barbecue and set aside to rest, loosely covered, for about 5 minutes. Sprinkle with salt and serve with lemon wedges and tzatziki salad.

Serves 4

Moroccan lamb fillets with spicy eggplant

PREP **25 mins**   MARINATE **2 hrs**   COOK **4–5 mins**   REST **5 mins**

There's plenty of confusion about the difference between fillets and backstraps or loins on lambs. If you look at a short loin chop, I reckon that the fillet is the smaller, super tender piece and the backstrap or loin is the larger, still very lean piece. Both are delicious and work perfectly in this recipe; you will just have to adjust the cooking time for the bigger piece of meat.

8–12 lamb fillets, silver sinew removed, or 3–4 loins or backstraps, trimmed of all fat and sinew
cous cous, to serve (optional)

MARINADE
1 teaspoon paprika
1 tablespoon ground cumin
1 teaspoon ground coriander
2 cloves garlic, crushed
2 tablespoons parsley, very finely chopped
zest of 1 lemon
⅓ cup (80 ml) olive oil

SPICY EGGPLANT
1 large or 2 medium eggplants
1 tablespoon salt
2 cloves garlic, crushed
½–1 teaspoon chilli flakes
2 tablespoons red-wine vinegar
2 tablespoons olive oil

1 Combine the marinade ingredients in a shallow glass or ceramic bowl and add the lamb, turning to coat thoroughly. Cover with plastic film and leave in the fridge to marinate for 2 hours.
2 To make the spicy eggplant, cut the eggplant into 1 cm slices crossways and place in a colander. Sprinkle with the salt to remove some moisture (and alleged bitterness – I'm not sure) and leave for 20 minutes. Wipe clean with a slightly damp paper towel.
3 Combine all the other spicy eggplant ingredients in a small bowl and set aside.
4 Bring the meat to room temperature by removing from the fridge half an hour before cooking. Cook the lamb and eggplant side by side, on a preheated chargrill or flat grillplate over high heat for about 4–5 minutes, or until done to your liking. Remove the lamb and eggplant from the grill and set the lamb aside to rest, loosely covered, for about 5 minutes.
5 Slice the lamb fillets, then divide the eggplant between four serving plates and place sliced lamb fillets on each, pouring over any juices from the resting process. Serve with a little cous cous if you like.

Serves 4

107

< Lamb racks with roasted baby carrots

PREP **10** mins   COOK **30–40** mins   REST **10** mins

A trick to making this fast and easy: have your barbecue working like a screaming hot oven, but with no heat directly under the baking dish. I suggest that you trim the lamb racks so that they cook more quickly – add another 15 minutes if you use racks with a full cover of fat.

2 × 8 bone lamb racks, trimmed of all fat and sinew
⅓ cup (80 ml) olive oil
sea salt and freshly ground black pepper
3 bunches of (preferably different-coloured)
  baby carrots, peeled or scrubbed well
4 garlic cloves, halved
1 tablespoon thyme or rosemary leaves
2 tablespoons olive oil
sea salt, to taste

1 Bring the lamb racks to room temperature by removing from the fridge half an hour before cooking, and halve them to make serving easier. Rub racks with a little oil and season well with salt and pepper.
2 Put the oil in a large, non-stick baking dish and add the carrots, garlic cloves and thyme or rosemary leaves. Toss to coat and sprinkle salt on top. Place lamb racks on top of the carrots, pushing down so they touch the bottom of the dish.
3 Place the baking dish in the middle of a very hot barbecue with heat surrounding it on both sides, but not directly underneath. Close the hood and cook for about 15–20 minutes, until the lamb is medium–rare or done to your liking. Remove the lamb to a warm bowl and set aside to rest, loosely covered, for about 10 minutes.
4 Continue cooking the carrots for another 15–20 minutes until slightly crunchy and caramelised, then remove from the barbecue. Either place them in a serving bowl and return lamb racks to the baking dish and place both dishes in the middle of the table, or place a rack of four cutlets and several carrots onto each (warm) serving plate.

Serves 4

Forequarter chops with barbecue sauce

PREP **25** mins   MARINATE **4–12** hrs   COOK **13–20** mins   REST **5** mins

I wanted to include a couple of lamb rib recipes (because they're just delicious) but they just don't fit in a fast and easy book onaccounta they really need to cook slowly for a couple of hours. Solution? Good, old-fashioned forequarter chops, which give you the sweetness of meat on the bone, but don't need slow cooking. Encourage your family and friends to eat these with their fingers; there really is no other way.

8 lamb forequarter chops
coleslaw or potato salad, to serve

MARINADE
1 teaspoon ground sweet paprika
½ teaspoon ground cayenne pepper
1 teaspoon celery salt
2 cloves garlic, crushed or grated
½ teaspoon onion powder
1 teaspoon sea salt
½ teaspoon freshly ground black pepper
½ cup lemon juice (juice from 2 lemons)
½ cup Worcestershire sauce
1 cup cider vinegar

BARBECUE SAUCE
1½ cups (375 ml) tomato sauce
⅓ cup (80 ml) water
1 teaspoon mustard powder
¼ cup (60 ml) cider vinegar
1 tablespoon lemon juice
1½ tablespoons brown sugar

1 Combine the marinade ingredients in a shallow glass or ceramic bowl and add the lamb chops, turning to coat thoroughly. Cover with plastic film and leave in the fridge to marinate for 4–12 hours.
2 Bring the meat to room temperature by removing from the fridge half an hour before cooking.
3 To make the sauce, combine all ingredients in a saucepan and bring to the boil, then reduce over low to medium heat for 5 minutes.
4 Cook the chops on a lightly oiled flat grillplate over medium heat for about 10–15 minutes, or until done to your liking. Brush the chops very liberally with the barbecue sauce and cook for 3–4 minutes more. Remove chops from the grill and set aside to rest, loosely covered, for about 5 minutes.
5 Serve with coleslaw or potato salad.

Serves 4

LAMB

109

Piri Piri butterflied spatchcock >

PREP **10 mins**   MARINATE **4–12 hrs**   COOK **20–25 mins**   REST **5 mins**

Instead of dry, nasty takeaway jobbies, have a crack at these at home and see what a wonderful, tender, spicy result you get. I'm using good-sized spatchcock instead of full-size chooks only because they'll cook faster.

You never want to baste cooked chicken with the same marinade that has touched raw chicken, as bacteria may develop. I suggest that after you have made the marinade you set aside about a third to brush on as the chooks cook.

If you can start this a day ahead and leave the birds to marinate for 12 hours, the flavours will be even better.

4 × spatchcocks, butterflied (you could ask your poultry supplier to do this for you)
lemon halves, to serve

MARINADE
8 cloves garlic, chopped
3–4 cm piece ginger, grated or finely sliced
large handful of coriander leaves
1 tablespoon dried chilli flakes
1 tablespoon paprika
1 teaspoon cayenne pepper, optional
1 teaspoon sea salt
1 teaspoon freshly ground black pepper
1 cup (250 ml) olive oil

1 To butterfly the spatchcock yourself, use a sharp knife to cut through the cavity, either side of the backbone, discard the backbone then flatten the bird out with a heavy knife. Make a couple of slashes across the thickest parts of the flesh.
2 Place all the marinade ingredients in a food processor and blend to a smooth paste.
3 Place the spatchcocks in a shallow glass or ceramic bowl and pour over two-thirds of the marinade, turning the birds to coat evenly, pushing the marinade into the slashes in the breast. Reserve the last one-third of marinade to baste the spatchcocks with as they cook. Cover with plastic film and leave in the fridge to marinate for at least 4 hours (or up to 12 hours if you can).
4 Bring the spatchcocks to room temperature by removing from the fridge half an hour before cooking.
5 Cook on a preheated medium chargrill, brushing occasionally with the reserved marinade, for 20–25 minutes or until the juices from the thickest part of the thigh run clear when pierced with a skewer. Set aside to rest, loosely covered, for about 5 minutes. Serve with lemon halves.

Serves 4

Pork and fennel rissoles

PREP 10 mins   COOK 6–8 mins

A nice, easy recipe. The flavours just work, and make sure you have enough for leftovers, school lunches, snacks, whatever. Trust me, there will be plenty of demand for them.

600 g pork mince
2 cloves garlic, grated
1 small onion, grated or minced in a food processor
1 tablespoon fennel seeds, lightly crushed in
   a mortar and pestle
1 teaspoon salt
½ teaspoon freshly ground black pepper
1 cup (70 g) panko breadcrumbs or coarse
   breadcrumbs made from stale white bread
2 eggs
1 tablespoon flat-leaf parsley, finely chopped
olive oil, for pan-frying
tzatziki (see recipe for Cumin Lamb Cutlets with Tzatziki
   Salad page 106) and a green salad, to serve

1 Place all the ingredients (except the oil) in a large bowl and mix very thoroughly with your hands. Shape into rissoles about 4–6 cm by 1–2 cm.
2 Cook on a preheated oiled flat grillplate over medium heat for 3–4 minutes each side or until nicely golden and cooked through.
3 Serve with tzatziki and a sharply dressed green salad.

Serves 4

Marinated chicken thighs with salsa salad >

PREP 15 mins   MARINATE 2–4 hrs   COOK 20–25 mins   REST 5 mins

Here's a recipe that I was cooking back in the '80s. The marinade for the chook is very simple, and its accompaniment is sort of a salsa and sort of a salad, so we'll call it both. Not trying to be clever here, but it does make a yummy weekend lunch.

8 chicken thigh fillets, skin on, trimmed of excess fat
sea salt
lemon wedges, to serve
crusty bread, to serve (optional)

MARINADE
8 sprigs thyme, leaves picked
1 red chilli, seeded and finely sliced
⅓ cup (80 ml) olive oil
¼ cup (60 ml) lemon juice
½ teaspoon freshly ground black pepper
1 teaspoon honey

SALSA SALAD
300 g butternut pumpkin, peeled and cut into 2 cm pieces
1 tablespoon olive oil
2 tablespoons red-wine vinegar
sea salt and freshly ground black pepper
large handful flat-leaf parsley leaves, very roughly chopped
2 tomatoes, seeded and finely diced
1 red capsicum, white insides and seeds removed,
   finely diced
1 spring onion, white and pale-green parts only,
   sliced diagonally
½–1 red chilli, seeded and finely sliced

1 Combine the marinade ingredients in a shallow glass or ceramic bowl and add the chicken pieces, turning to coat thoroughly. Cover with plastic film and leave in the fridge to marinate for 2–4 hours.
2 Bring the chicken to room temperature by removing from the fridge half an hour before cooking.
3 To make the salsa salad, boil or steam the pumpkin for 10 minutes until al dente, then set aside to cool to room temperature. Mix together the oil and vinegar in a large salad bowl and season with salt and pepper. Add the pumpkin, fold through the remaining ingredients and set aside.
4 Cook chicken on a preheated chargrill over medium–high heat about 5–8 minutes each side until the outside is scorched and the juices run clear. Set aside to rest, loosely covered, for about 5 minutes.
5 Season with salt before serving alongside the salsa salad with lemon wedges and some crusty bread if you like.

Serves 4

CHICKEN & PORK

Baked parmesan chicken

PREP **15 mins**   COOK **30 mins**

This is another dish that you could easily cook indoors in the oven, but then you wouldn't get to stand in the fresh air, in need of a cold drink, supervising the barbie.

The best thing about this recipe is that it is nearly impossible to screw up the cooking as the chicken stays beautifully moist by absorbing all the liquid.

Chicken supreme is breast of chicken with the wing bone attached.

1½ tablespoons pine nuts
150 g butter
2 cloves garlic, finely chopped
2 golden shallots, peeled and finely chopped
6 sprigs thyme, leaves removed
1 tablespoon flat-leaf parsley, finely chopped
⅓ cup (25 g) finely grated parmesan
sea salt and freshly ground black pepper, to taste
4 chicken supremes
1 cup (250 ml) white wine
1 cup (250 ml) chicken stock
mashed or roast potatoes, to serve

1 Lightly toast the pine nuts in a dry non-stick frying pan over high heat for a couple of minutes, watching closely so that they don't burn, until they are golden-brown. Set aside.

2 Heat 100 g of the butter in a frying pan over low heat and cook the garlic and golden shallots until they are soft, then add the thyme leaves and parsley. Add the pine nuts and half the parmesan, stirring to combine, and season well with salt and pepper. Allow mixture to cool so the butter begins to solidify.

3 Gently insert your first two fingers under the skin of each chicken breast and ease it from the flesh. Insert a quarter of the butter mixture under the skin and pull the skin back into place. Place chicken skin-side up in a roasting pan just big enough to hold it all.

4 Pour the wine and stock over the chicken, sprinkle with the remaining parmesan and season again with salt and pepper. Place the baking dish in the middle of the barbecue with heat surrounding it on both sides, but not directly underneath. Close the hood and cook for half an hour over high heat, until the juices run clear when the meat near the bone is pierced. Remove the chicken from the pan and place it on a plate in a warm place. Remove pan from the heat and whisk through the rest of the butter.

5 Serve the chicken with the sauce on the side and mashed or roast potatoes.

Serves 4

< Balinese pork

PREP 10 mins   COOK 35 mins

The basic ingredients in this classic Balinese braise are plenty of garlic, ginger, shallots and kecap manis (an Indonesian sweet soy sauce) – and, of course, pork.

You can cut the pork into bigger pieces, say 2–3 cm cubes, and cook it for an hour or more, or stick to this recipe and let it simmer for about half an hour. If you're really pressed for time, leave out the chicken stock and make it a very quick stir-fry.

2 tablespoons neutral oil
500–600 g lean pork belly, cut into pieces
   of 3 cm × 1 cm
2 cloves garlic, sliced
3–4 cm piece ginger, peeled and very finely sliced
6 golden shallots, peeled and sliced
up to 12 whole bird's eye chillies for the brave;
   1 red chilli, sliced, for weasels like me
½ teaspoon freshly ground black pepper
⅓ cup (80 ml) kecap manis
2 tablespoons light soy sauce
1 cup (250 ml) chicken stock

1 Place the oil in a wok and, when hot, add the pork belly, stirring occasionally for a few minutes while it browns. Add the garlic, ginger, shallots, chillies and black pepper and stir for another minute to soften pork, then add the kecap manis and soy sauce, stirring so the pork is well coated.
2 Add the stock and reduce heat to a simmer for about half an hour until the pork is tender and nearly all the liquid has been absorbed. You may need to add more stock or water if the liquid reduces too quickly.
3 Serve immediately.

Serves 4

Apricot-glazed chicken with sultanas and pine nuts

PREP 15 mins   COOK 10 mins

Apologies to anyone old enough to remember the '70s, as this will doubtless bring back nightmares about every bachelor's only dish: Apricot Chicken, made with a can of apricots and a packet of dehydrated chicken soup, a chicken and not a lot else.

Hopefully this recipe is a bit different.

4 boneless, skinless chicken thighs, trimmed
   of excess fat
2 tablespoons apricot jam
1 tablespoon sultanas
1 tablespoon pine nuts
2 tablespoons panko breadcrumbs or coarse
   breadcrumbs made from stale white bread
2 tablespoons neutral oil

1 Place the chicken thighs on a board, and evenly spread half the jam over one side.
2 Mix together the sultanas, pine nuts and breadcrumbs and divide between the four thighs, placing the stuffing in a strip along one side. Roll up the thighs to enclose the stuffing and secure with one or two toothpicks, or kitchen string (not the plastic-coated sort).
3 Cook on a preheated oiled flat grillplate over low–medium heat for 10 minutes, placing some foil over the top to help cook them evenly. They are ready when the juices run clear when tested with a skewer.
4 As soon as they're cooked, brush with the remaining jam (be quick, it will burn) and serve immediately.

Serves 4

CHICKEN & PORK

Tea-smoked quail

PREP **15 mins**   COOK **10–12 mins**

There's a nicely paced two-step process to this dish. First, smoke the quail, then finish cooking them on the grill. As you are cooking the quail, stir-fry the bean shoots in the wok you used to smoke the quail. Easy as.

Oolong tea is semi-fermented tea, somewhere between green tea and black tea, and known for its health benefits. You should be able to find it in specialty tea shops or in Asian grocers.

2 tablespoons jasmine or oolong tea
2 tablespoons rice
2 tablespoons brown sugar
4 large quail, butterflied (you could ask your poultry
   supplier to do this for you)
¼ cup (60 ml) neutral oil
sea salt
1 tablespoon dark soy sauce
2 tablespoons honey
1 teaspoon sesame oil
½ teaspoon dried chilli flakes
2 spring onions, white and pale-green parts only,
   cut into 1 cm lengths
1 clove garlic, grated or finely chopped
3 cups (240 g) bean sprouts
1 tablespoon light soy sauce

1 Line a large wok with a couple of layers of foil and add the tea, rice and sugar.
2 To butterfly the quail yourself, use a sharp knife to cut through the cavity, either side of the backbone, with a heavy knife, discard the backbone then flatten the bird out.
3 Brush the quail on both sides with 1 tablespoon of the neutral oil and season the cut side with a little salt. Place, skin-side up, on a circular rack that will fit in the wok.
4 Place the wok on the highest heat over the wok burner. When the mixture begins to smoke, add the rack with the quail, then cover with a tight-fitting lid and smoke for 5 minutes.
5 Meanwhile, combine the dark soy sauce, honey, sesame oil and chilli flakes in a small saucepan over low heat until melted (or cheat and do this in a microwave).
6 Remove the quail from the rack and brush them well with the honey and soy mixture. Place on a lightly greased, very hot grillplate for 1–2 minutes on each side to brown them, taking care that the honey doesn't burn.
7 While the quail is cooking, remove the foil, wipe the wok clean and add the remaining neutral oil. Place over high heat and stir-fry the spring onion and garlic for about 30 seconds, then add the bean sprouts and quickly toss. Pour in the light soy sauce and cook for 30 seconds.
8 Immediately transfer bean sprouts to a serving platter, top with the quail and serve.

Serves 4

Middle Eastern spatchcock
with cinnamon and chilli pumpkin

PREP **15 mins**   MARINATE **30 mins–1 hr**   COOK **25 mins**   REST **5 mins**

This marinade recipe was in *The Great Aussie Family Cookbook,* and is worth repeating here, this time pairing it with spatchcock and lovely sweet pumpkin.

The birds are just the right size to absorb all the marinade flavours and to cook quickly on the barbie without drying out. If you prefer, use 2 small chooks instead.

4 small spatchcock, butterflied (you could ask your poultry supplier to do this for you)

MARINADE
zest and juice of one lime
2 cloves garlic, crushed or grated
2 teaspoons sea salt
120 ml olive oil
1 tablespoon ground cumin
1 tablespoon ground coriander
1 teaspoon ground cinnamon
1 teaspoon ground turmeric
1 tablespoon sweet paprika
1 teaspoon ground cardamom
½ teaspoon cayenne pepper (optional)
lime wedges, to serve

CINNAMON AND CHILLI PUMPKIN
½ large butternut pumpkin, seeds discarded
2 tablespoons olive oil
2 teaspoons ground cinnamon
½ teaspoon salt
½ teaspoon cayenne pepper

1 Dry the spatchcocks' skin with a paper towel. Combine the marinade ingredients in a shallow glass or ceramic bowl and add the spatchcocks, turning to coat thoroughly. If possible, force a little marinade between the breast meat and the skin. Cover with plastic film and leave in the fridge to marinate for half to 1 hour.
2 To make the cinnamon and chilli pumpkin, slice the pumpkin into 1 cm slices crossways, leaving the skin on if you like. Brush with the olive oil and dust with the combined cinnamon, salt and pepper.
3 Bring the spatchcocks to room temperature by removing from the fridge half an hour before cooking, then place skin-side down on preheated hot chargrill. At the same time, place the pumpkin slices on the chargrill. Reduce the heat immediately and close the lid. Turn spatchcocks after 10 minutes, then cook for another 15 minutes. Turn pumpkin slices once.
4 Test spatchcocks for done-ness by inserting a skewer or point of a sharp knife into the thickest part – if the juices run clear, they're done. Set aside to rest in a large bowl, loosely covered, for 5 minutes before serving.
5 Serve the spatchcock, with juices drizzled over the top, with the pumpkin slices and lime wedges.

Serves 4 generously

121

Caribbean chicken with corn relish

PREP **15 mins**   MARINATE **4–12 hrs**   COOK **40 mins**   REST **5 mins**

Some lovely big flavours in this dish. It would traditionally be served with rice and beans, but let's keep things simple.

The corn relish can be served with just about anything on the barbie – fish, chicken, pork or the plainest of steaks.

8 boneless chicken thighs, preferably with skin on
lime halves, to serve

MARINADE
zest of 1 lime
zest of ½ orange
¼ cup (60 ml) orange juice
¼ cup (60 ml) lime juice
1 teaspoon allspice
3–4 cm piece ginger, grated
1 clove garlic, grated or crushed
1 teaspoon dried oregano
½ small red onion, chopped
1 jalapeno chilli, seeded and chopped
2 tablespoons olive oil

CORN RELISH
2 big cobs of corn, or 3 smaller ones
2 tablespoons neutral oil
1 clove garlic, crushed or finely chopped
4 golden shallots, finely chopped
1½–2 cm piece ginger, peeled and grated
½ red capsicum, white insides and seeds removed,
**   cut into 1 cm pieces**
½ green capsicum, white insides and seeds removed,
**   cut into 1 cm pieces**
1 large tomato, seeded and diced
1 jalapeno chilli, seeded and finely diced
2 tablespoons brown sugar
3 tablespoons cider vinegar
1 teaspoon Tabasco sauce, more to taste
sea salt and freshly ground black pepper, to taste
handful coriander leaves, roughly chopped

1 To make the marinade, combine all marinade ingredients in a food processor and blend to a smooth paste. Place the chicken pieces in a bowl with the marinade, turning to coat thoroughly. Cover with plastic film and leave in the fridge to marinate for 4–12 hours. Bring the chicken to room temperature by removing from the fridge half an hour before cooking.

2 To make the corn relish, bring a large saucepan of water to the boil, add the corn and cook, covered, for 10–15 minutes or until the corn is tender. Gently remove the corn from the pot and transfer to a plate. Once cool enough to handle, stand each corn cob up on a chopping board and carefully slice the kernels off with a large knife. Set aside.

3 Heat the oil in a deep-sided frying pan, wok or saucepan, then add the garlic, shallots and ginger and cook over medium heat for a few minutes until soft. Add the capsicums, tomato, chilli and corn kernels and stir for another couple of minutes until they soften slightly. Stir through the sugar, vinegar, Tabasco, salt and pepper and bring to the boil, then reduce heat and simmer sauce for about 10 minutes, stirring occasionally. Taste to check whether it needs more vinegar or sugar (or Tabasco, if you're game) then stir through the coriander leaves and transfer to a serving bowl or jar.

4 Cook the chicken on a lightly oiled chargrill or flat grillplate over medium heat for about 4–5 minutes on each side. Set aside to rest, loosely covered, for about 5 minutes.

5 Serve with a large spoonful of the relish and lime halves.

Serves 4

Teriyaki chicken

PREP **25 mins**   MARINATE **1 hr**   COOK **8–10 mins**

It might be very mainstream Japanese, but this is a dish that the whole family loves, and it is great for weeknight barbecues. Of course, you could cook it inside, but it can get a bit smoky and smelly. I used this recipe in *The Great Aussie Family Cookbook*, but it works particularly well on the barbie so is worth repeating.

All you need are some Asian greens like choy sum, bok choy or even snake beans to round out the meal.

**750 g boneless chicken thigh fillets,
  skin on, trimmed of excess fat**
1 tablespoon neutral oil
steamed rice and Asian greens, to serve

MARINADE
1 teaspoon finely grated ginger
⅓ cup (80 ml) shoyu (Japanese soy sauce)
⅓ cup (80 ml) mirin
1 tablespoon sugar
2 tablespoons sake

1 Combine the marinade ingredients in a small bowl or jug. Place the chicken in a shallow glass or ceramic bowl and pour over two-thirds of the marinade, turning to coat thoroughly. Reserve the last one-third of the marinade to baste the chicken as it cooks. Cover with plastic film and leave in the fridge to marinate for 1 hour.
2 Bring the chicken to room temperature by removing from the fridge half an hour before cooking, then drain it.
3 Heat the oil in the baking tray of your barbecue, in a wok with a lid on the wok burner, or even on the flat grillplate if you have a large lid to place over part of it. Add the chicken, skin-side down, and cook over medium–high heat for 4–5 minutes or until the skin is nicely golden.
4 Turn the thighs over and baste with the reserved marinade. Cover with a lid, then reduce the heat to low and cook for 4–5 minutes or until the chicken is cooked through and the juices run clear when the thickest part is pierced with a skewer. Remove the lid and continue cooking over low heat until the sauce thickens.
5 Remove the chicken and cut into slices. Spoon over the sauce and serve with steamed rice and Asian greens.

Serves 4

Pineapple-glazed pork chops >

PREP **10 mins**   COOK **8–10 mins**

Here's a great way to tart up some plain pork chops. It only takes a few minutes to throw together and you're likely to have all the ingredients in the kitchen cupboard – unless your mates drank all the rum, as they do.

4 pork loin chops
½ pineapple, peeled, cored and 'eyes' removed, sliced
2 tablespoons neutral oil
sea salt and freshly ground black pepper
baby rocket leaves, to serve

SALAD DRESSING
2 tablespoons olive oil
1 tablespoon white-wine vinegar
sea salt and freshly ground black pepper, to serve

GLAZE
40 g butter
2 cloves garlic, crushed
2 tablespoons pineapple juice
2 tablespoons dark rum
2 tablespoons tomato sauce
1 tablespoon lemon juice
½ cup (110 g) brown sugar
large pinch dried chilli flakes, or more to taste
freshly ground black pepper

1 To make the glaze, melt the butter in a small saucepan, then add the garlic and cook for 2 minutes over low heat without allowing it to brown. Add all the other ingredients, bring to the boil, and simmer over low heat for a couple of minutes then remove from the heat and set aside.
2 Brush both sides of the pork chops and pineapple slices with the oil.
3 Place the chops on a preheated flat grillplate, seasoning with a little salt and pepper, and cook over high heat for 2 minutes. Turn the chops after 1 minute, when the second side is half done, and transfer to the chargrill along with the pineapple slices.
4 Brush the pork and the pineapple with the rest of the glaze on both sides, and cook for another 5 minutes or so on each side, allowing them to brown.
5 To make the salad dressing, mix all the ingredients together in a large salad bowl. Toss through the rocket, mixing well.
6 Transfer the pork and pineapple to plates and serve with the rocket.

Serves 4

Chinese chicken skewers

PREP 10 mins   MARINATE 2–4 hrs   COOK 10 mins

Pretty well Chinese Flavours 101 here, but nothing wrong with that. The sweet and salty flavours make these perfect for young palates, as well as some older ones. I'd make these for the kids and the grandparents and something more interesting for the in-betweens.

6 boneless, skinless chicken thighs, trimmed of excess fat and cut into 2–3 cm pieces
2 spring onions, white and pale-green parts only, cut into 2 cm pieces
steamed rice and Chinese greens, to serve

MARINADE
1 clove garlic, crushed
3–4 cm piece ginger, peeled and grated
¼ cup (60 ml) hoisin sauce
1 tablespoon tomato sauce
1 tablespoon light soy sauce

1 Combine the garlic, ginger, hoisin sauce, tomato sauce and soy sauce in a shallow glass or ceramic bowl and add the chicken, turning to coat thoroughly. Cover with plastic film and leave to marinate in the fridge for 2–4 hours.
2 Bring the chicken to room temperature by removing from the fridge half an hour before cooking.
3 Thread the chicken and spring onion onto skewers and cook on a preheated chargrill over low–medium heat for about 10 minutes, turning occasionally, until just cooked through.
4 Serve with steamed rice and Chinese greens.

Serves 4

Pork medallions with maple butter >

PREP 10 mins   COOK 5 mins

Too, too easy.
   No marinating required, maybe 5 minutes to make the butter and about the same to cook the pork. Of course you could use last week's butter that you froze and reduce the time even further. Great with the Corny Coleslaw in the picture (see page 180).

1 thick pork fillet (approx 500 g), shiny silver sinew removed with a sharp knife, fillet cut into 1½ cm thick slices
sea salt and freshly ground black pepper
1 tablespoon olive oil

MAPLE BUTTER
100 g butter, chopped into 1 cm cubes
finely grated zest of ½ lemon
1 tablespoon pure maple syrup
1 teaspoon thyme leaves

1 To make the maple butter, place all the ingredients in a small bowl and mash with the back of a fork until completely combined. Place a sheet of baking paper on your workbench, with the butter in the centre. Use your hands to shape butter into a cylinder, then roll and twist the ends of the paper to make a bon bon. Refrigerate until ready to use, and cut into ½ cm thick discs as required.
2 Brush the medallions with oil and season with a little salt and plenty of pepper.
3 Cook on a preheated flat grillplate or chargrill for a couple of minutes on each side.
4 Transfer to serving plates and place a disc of butter on top.

Serves 4

CHICKEN & PORK

Asian-marinated pork chops

PREP 10 mins   MARINATE 4–12 hrs   COOK 8–10 mins

Let's take a pan-Asian approach here, which is a nice way of saying that the recipe isn't authentically anything in particular, just a combination of things you might have in the cupboard at home. Doesn't matter a bit because the flavour is familiar and delicious. You could also use this marinade with chicken, or seafood.

   You could make a really simple fried rice out of cooked rice (easiest if you have some frozen), spring onions, omelette and soy sauce to go with these.

**4 × 250 g meaty pork chops, ideally with
   some marbling through the meat
2 tablespoons neutral oil
fried rice, to serve (optional)
steamed choy sum with oyster sauce,
   to serve (optional)**

MARINADE
**½ cup (125 ml) mirin
½ cup (125 ml) light soy sauce
1 teaspoon sesame oil
2 tablespoons brown sugar
2 cloves garlic, crushed or grated
3–4 cm piece ginger, peeled and grated
2 spring onions, white and pale-green parts only,
   very finely chopped**

1 To make the marinade, combine all the ingredients in a shallow glass or ceramic bowl and add the pork chops, turning to coat thoroughly. Cover with plastic film and leave in the fridge to marinate for 4–12 hours.
2 Bring the chops to room temperature by removing from the fridge half an hour before cooking. Drain off any excess marinade and cook them on a lightly oiled flat grillplate over medium–high heat for 4–5 minutes on each side, depending on thickness, or until just cooked through.
3 Transfer to plates and serve with fried rice and/or steamed choy sum with oyster sauce.

Serves 4

Five-spice pork belly

PREP 15 mins   MARINATE 12–24 hrs   COOK 25 mins

The great thing about pork belly is that it's so delicious.

   The problem with pork belly is that it takes hours to cook properly in a whole piece.

   My solution is to slice it quite thinly, give it a simple Asian marinade and cook it in not much time at all. The result? Try it for yourself and see.

   For best results, start this a day ahead.

**700 g pork belly, skin removed, cut across
   the grain into 1 cm thick slices
2 large handfuls of watercress leaves and
   thin stems
1 tablespoon neutral oil
1 teaspoon soy sauce
1 tablespoon mirin
sea salt and freshly ground black pepper,
   to taste**

MARINADE
**2 tablespoons neutral oil
2 cloves garlic, crushed or grated
1½–2 cm piece ginger, peeled and grated
1 tablespoon five-spice powder
1 scant teaspoon Sichuan peppercorns,
   ground in a mortar and pestle
1 teaspoon salt
½ teaspoon sugar**

1 To make the marinade, combine all the ingredients in a shallow glass or ceramic bowl. Add the pork, turning to coat thoroughly. Cover with plastic film and leave to marinate in the fridge for 12–24 hours.
2 Bring the pork to room temperature by removing from the fridge half an hour before cooking.
3 Cook the pork on a preheated chargrill over medium–low heat for 25 minutes, turning occasionally, moving it to the flat grillplate if it begins to flame and burn.
4 Meanwhile, combine the watercress, oil, soy sauce and mirin in a salad bowl and toss to combine. Taste and season with salt and pepper, if needed.
5 Stack the pork strips on a plate and serve the salad beside them.

Serves 4

Seared duck breast with wok-fried noodles

PREP **15 mins**   MARINATE **2 hrs**   COOK **6–10 mins**

Ducks is tricky creatures. You need to slow cook the legs and thighs to get them tender, but the breasts are best served at least rosy – in France they would be blood rare. Luckily, we can buy the breasts separately these days while the marylands go off to every restaurant in the country to be turned into confit.

As there is a lot of fat under the skin, try scoring the skin to let as much escape as possible.

If using dried noodles, follow the instructions on the packet for soaking times.

4 duck breasts, trimmed of any fat

MARINADE
1 teaspoon ground cinnamon
1 teaspoon five-spice powder
½ teaspoon ground star anise
1 tablespoon honey
1 teaspoon finely grated orange zest
2 tablespoons orange juice
1 tablespoon neutral oil

NOODLES
½ carrot, cut into 2 cm long matchsticks
1 tablespoon neutral oil
1 clove garlic, crushed
2 spring onions, white or pale-green parts only,
  cut into 2 cm long matchsticks (or ½ bunch
  garlic chives, cut into 2 cm lengths)
1 cup (80 g) bean sprouts
100 g fresh or dried egg noodles
  (soaked and drained, if dried)
1 tablespoon light soy sauce
½ teaspoon sesame oil
1 teaspoon sesame seeds

1 Place the marinade ingredients in a shallow glass or ceramic bowl. Score the skin on the duck breasts in a criss-cross pattern, then add to the bowl, turning to coat thoroughly. Cover with plastic film and leave in the fridge to marinate for 2 hours.
2 Bring the duck to room temperature by removing it from the fridge half an hour before cooking.
3 Cook the duck on a preheated flat grillplate over medium–high heat for 3–5 minutes, then turn and cook the other side for 3–4 minutes or until cooked to medium, or done to your liking. Transfer to a plate and rest, loosely covered, for 5 minutes.
4 To make the noodles, blanch the carrot in boiling water for 30 seconds, then drain.
5 Heat the oil in a wok over high heat. When hot, add the garlic, spring onion and carrot and cook for 30 seconds. Add the bean sprouts and noodles and toss to heat through. Pour in the soy sauce and stir to coat, then add the sesame oil. Transfer to a serving dish and sprinkle with the sesame seeds.
6 Serve immediately with the duck breasts, sliced.

Serves 4

CHICKEN & PORK

Quail yakitori with radicchio salad

PREP 15 mins   MARINATE 2–4 hrs   COOK 5 mins

The 'normal' yakitori that we see everywhere from shopping centre food courts to fine dining restaurants is made with chicken.

I've tried it with duck breasts, cooking them slowly so the layer of fat under the skin melts, but they're still a bit fatty. Quail just might be the answer. More flavour than chook and virtually no fat. You can buy the breast-only portions at supermarkets these days.

400 g (20–24) quail breast fillets, left whole or
cut into 2 cm pieces
6–8 spring onions, white and pale-green parts only,
cut into 2–3 cm pieces

MARINADE
⅓ cup (80 ml) shoyu (Japanese soy sauce)
¼ cup (60 ml) sake
2 tablespoons mirin
1 tablespoon sugar

RADICCHIO SALAD
1 tablespoon pine nuts
1 tablespoon neutral oil
1 tablespoon mirin
1 tablespoon rice vinegar
sea salt
1 head radicchio, trimmed, leaves finely shredded
1 small stalk celery, sliced
½ small carrot, coarsely shredded

1 Lightly toast the pine nuts in a dry non-stick frying pan over high heat for a couple of minutes, watching closely so they don't burn, until they are golden-brown. Set aside.
2 Combine the marinade ingredients in a small bowl or jug. Place the quail fillets in a shallow glass or ceramic bowl and pour over two-thirds of the marinade, turning to coat thoroughly. Reserve the last one-third of the marinade to baste the quail fillets with as they cook. Cover with plastic film and leave in the fridge to marinate for 2–4 hours.
3 Bring quail to room temperature by removing from the fridge half an hour before cooking, then thread the quail and spring onion pieces alternately onto eight skewers and set aside.
4 To make the salad, combine the neutral oil, mirin, rice vinegar and a pinch of salt in a bowl, then toss through the other ingredients.
5 Grill the skewers on a preheated chargrill over medium heat, turning occasionally, for 5 minutes or until just cooked through. Brush some of the reserved marinade over the skewers during the first couple of minutes of cooking only (to allow it time to cook).
6 Serve two skewers per person with a spoonful of salad.

Serves 4 as a light meal

CHICKEN & PORK

Butter chicken skewers

PREP **15 mins**   MARINATE **4–24 hrs**   COOK **15–20 mins**

Yep, this is every family's favourite Indian takeaway dish, except it's on sticks, and cooked on the barbecue. Tastes even better if you start it the day before.

You can cook the chicken on the chargrill and the sauce on the wok burner, if your brain still works well enough to do two things at once (I struggle).

800 g boneless chicken thighs or breasts,
  cut into 3–4 cm pieces
about 18 cashew nuts
⅓ cup (80 ml) neutral oil
1 small onion, very finely chopped
1 cinnamon stick
1 teaspoon salt
1 teaspoon sweet paprika
½ teaspoon ground chilli powder (optional)
2 tablespoons tomato paste
1 cup (250 ml) pouring cream or pure thick
  (not thickened) cream
1 bay leaf, preferably fresh
basmati rice, to serve

MARINADE
100 g plain natural yoghurt
2 garlic cloves, crushed or grated
1½–2 cm piece ginger, grated
1 teaspoon garam masala
1 teaspoon ground cumin
1 teaspoon ground turmeric

1 Combine the marinade ingredients in a shallow glass or ceramic bowl and add the chicken pieces, turning to coat thoroughly. Cover with plastic film and leave in the fridge to marinate for 4–24 hours.

2 To prepare the cashew nuts, dry fry them in a small dry frying pan over medium heat, shaking regularly until they brown. Grind 6 to a powder in a mortar and pestle, and reserve the rest.

3 Bring the chicken to room temperature by removing from the fridge half an hour before cooking. Thread the chicken pieces onto skewers. Heat half the oil on a preheated chargrill and start to fry the chicken skewers over high heat for about 1–2 minutes on each side, transferring them to the flat grillplate to finish cooking.

4 Heat the remaining oil in a deep-sided frying pan, wok or saucepan, then cook the onion over medium heat for a few minutes until soft.

5 Add the cinnamon stick, salt, paprika, chilli powder if using, tomato paste, cream and bay leaf to the onions and bring to the boil. Reduce heat and simmer sauce for 10 minutes then add the ground cashews. Cook for another few minutes, stirring occasionally, and add the whole cashews just before serving.

6 Place the chicken skewers onto plates and spoon the sauce over the top.

7 Serve with plain or saffron-coloured basmati rice.

Serves 4

Black pepper crab

PREP 10 mins   COOK 10–15 mins

If you're in Singapore and you want crab, it's either Black Pepper Crab or Chilli. I did a terrific simple Chilli Crab in *The Great Aussie Barbie Cookbook*, and a lovely complex one in *The Great Aussie Asian Cookbook*, so let's have a crack at Black Pepper Crab for a change.

It's a surprisingly straightforward dish, with ginger, garlic, dark and light soy, oyster sauce and, of course, the pepper – nothing exotic at all. If you were in Singapore, there's a good chance the crab would be deep-fried as the first stage of cooking, but we'll go for a slightly healthier approach.

Don't forget to select heavy crabs – the ones with plenty of meat in them.

⅓ cup (80 ml) neutral oil
1 large (1–1.5 kg) mud crab or 3 very large blue
   swimmer crabs, cleaned and cut into 6 pieces,
   shells and claws cracked with the back of a cleaver
50 g butter
4 cloves garlic, crushed or very finely chopped
3–4 cm piece ginger, peeled and grated
1 green chilli, seeded and very finely sliced
   (more to taste)
2 tablespoons oyster sauce
1 tablespoon light soy sauce
1 tablespoon dark soy sauce
1 teaspoon sugar
1 heaped tablespoon freshly ground black pepper
2 tablespoons water
large handful of coriander leaves, roughly chopped

1 Heat the oil in a lidded wok over high heat until hot, then, working in batches, add the crab pieces. Stir-fry the crab for 5 minutes until the shells turn orange – don't worry that the meat inside isn't cooked. Remove the crab to a large bowl and set aside.

2 Pour off all but 1 tablespoon of oil from the wok. Add the butter and, when melted, add the garlic, ginger and chilli. Cook over high heat for about 30 seconds until the mixture becomes aromatic, then add the oyster and soy sauces and the sugar.

3 Return the crab to the wok and stir well to coat with the sauce, then sprinkle over pepper and water, stirring again to coat. Bring to the boil and put lid on wok then reduce to a simmer. Simmer for 5–10 minutes until the meat is opaque, shaking the wok regularly to make sure the crab pieces cook evenly.

4 Once cooked, transfer to a serving platter and spoon the juices over. Top with coriander and serve immediately.

Serves 2

Chargrilled lobster with herb butter

PREP 20 mins   COOK approximately 10 mins

This is about as flash as you get on a barbecue. I love live lobsters. I bought one as a treat when I was first dating my wife thirty-odd years ago, but she heard it scraping around the polystyrene box in the back of the car and nearly had a fit.

A word of warning here – if you use a live lobster, you need to be prepared to kill it. The RSPCA has strict guidelines on how to kill a lobster humanely; (happily) you are no longer allowed to just plunge it alive into boiling water. First, you must render it insensible, and the best way to do that is to put it in the freezer for an hour (or you can send it out drinking with me). You can tell it is insensible when you can easily manipulate the abdomen or tail without resistance (same as me). Place the lobster on a chopping board and line a sharp, heavy-bladed knife up between its eyes. Insert the knife and, with one movement, bring the knife down through the head to the board. Cut the lobster into two pieces along its mid-line.

2 frozen lobster tails (about 200–300 g each),
   thawed in the fridge and halved or 1 live lobster
   (1–1.5 kg) halved and cleaned
2 tablespoons olive oil
sea salt and freshly ground black pepper, to taste
lemon wedges, to serve

HERB BUTTER
200 g butter, chopped into pieces and brought
   to room temperature
2 tablespoons parsley leaves, chopped
2 tablespoons basil leaves, torn
2 tablespoons chives, chopped
2 tablespoons oregano or marjoram leaves, chopped
1 teaspoon tomato paste
½ teaspoon fish sauce
1 teaspoon finely grated lemon zest
sea salt and freshly ground black pepper, to taste

1 To make the butter, combine all ingredients in a food processor and blend until smooth, or else just place them all in a bowl and mash with the back of a fork (more work but less washing up).
2 Place a sheet of baking paper on your workbench, with the butter in the centre. Use your hands to shape butter into a cylinder, then roll and twist the ends of the paper to make a bon bon. Refrigerate until ready to use.
3 Brush the flesh of the lobster with oil and season with salt and pepper. Cook the lobster halves, flesh-side down, on a chargrill over high heat for a few minutes. Turn the lobster halves over and cook on the shell side for a few more minutes until the flesh is nearly opaque. The exact time will depend on the size of the lobster.
4 Remove the roll of butter from the fridge, gently unroll it and slice butter into discs. Place a few discs of butter on top of each lobster half, and cook for another minute or so.
5 Serve very simply with lemon wedges and the rest of the butter on a plate at the table.

Serves 2

Chargrilled tuna with skordalia and parsley salad

PREP **20 mins**   COOK **20–25 mins**

You can make skordalia with bread or with spuds, most often with spuds. It's a lovely garlicky, lemony accompaniment to a whole range of barbecued meat and seafood.

Let's keep it simple here with a perfectly plain piece of tuna and a little salad of fresh herbs.

4 × 200–250 g tuna steaks
2 tablespoons olive oil

SKORDALIA
600 g desiree potatoes, peeled and quartered
6 cloves garlic, finely chopped
1 heaped teaspoon sea salt
⅔ cup (160 ml) olive oil
2 tablespoons lemon juice

SALAD
1 tablespoon olive oil
1 tablespoon lemon juice
sea salt and freshly ground black pepper, to taste
1 golden shallot, peeled and very finely sliced
large handful flat-leaf parsley leaves
handful oregano leaves

1 To make the salad, mix together the oil, lemon juice and salt and pepper to taste in a salad bowl. Toss through the shallot and herbs, mixing well. Set aside.
2 To make the skordalia, boil the potatoes in a saucepan in enough water to cover them for about 15–20 minutes, until they are cooked. Drain well and return them to the pan. Grind the garlic with the salt in a mortar and pestle until it forms a paste, then add to the potatoes. Otherwise, you could just grate the garlic into the potatoes. Add oil and lemon juice and mash until smooth. Taste and add more lemon juice if necessary.
3 Brush the tuna with olive oil and cook on a preheated chargrill over very high heat for about 1–2 minutes on each side, until it is medium–rare.
4 Place a big spoonful of skordalia on each plate and top with the tuna. Serve with a little salad on the side.

Serves 4

SEAFOOD

Blue eye with walnut sauce

PREP 15 mins   COOK 15–20 mins

I love simple sauces that add something special to a plain but perfect piece of fish – and take very little time and effort.

This easy walnut sauce also works really well with simply grilled chicken; just swap chicken stock for the fish stock.

4 × 200 g blue eye fillets, skin on
2 tablespoons olive oil
mashed or boiled potatoes or green vegetables,
    to serve

WALNUT SAUCE
100 g sugar
100 ml white-wine vinegar
2 tablespoons capers, very finely chopped
1 clove garlic, chopped
1½ cups (150 g) walnuts
½ cup (125 ml) extra virgin olive oil
¼ cup (60 ml) fish stock (optional)

1 To make the walnut sauce, place the sugar and vinegar in a saucepan and cook over high heat, stirring regularly until the sugar dissolves. Add the capers and simmer for 10 minutes.
2 While the sauce is simmering, place the garlic and walnuts in a food processor and pulse just until the walnuts are coarsely crushed – you don't want a fine paste.
3 Stir the walnut mixture into the sauce, then add the oil and fish stock, if using. Warm the sauce, stirring constantly; it doesn't need to boil. Add a little more oil or stock if it is too thick.
4 Heat the 2 tablespoons of oil in a heavy-based non-stick frying pan. Add the fish, skin-side down, and cook for 3–4 minutes on each side, depending on thickness, turning once, until just cooked through.
5 Transfer to serving plates before spooning the walnut sauce over the top. Serve with potatoes or green vegetables.

Serves 4

Tequila lime swordfish with salsa >

PREP 15 mins   MARINATE 15 mins   COOK 5 mins

This is a nice simple dish that combines the ceviche idea of 'cooking' seafood in lemon or lime juice and using it as a marinade before cooking the seafood.

The trick is not to leave it too long in the tequila and lime juice – about 15 minutes should do.

¼ cup (60 ml) tequila
¼ cup (60 ml) lime juice
¼ cup (60 ml) olive oil
2 cloves garlic, crushed
4 × 200–250 g pieces of swordfish
lime wedges, to serve (optional)

TOMATO SALSA
½ small red onion, chopped
2 tomatoes, seeded and diced
1 jalapeno chilli, seeded and finely diced
½ green capsicum, white insides and seeds
    removed, diced
2 tablespoons coriander leaves, chopped
1 tablespoon mint leaves, chopped
2 tablespoons olive oil
1 tablespoon lime juice
sea salt and freshly ground black pepper,
    to taste

1 Combine the tequila, lime juice, olive oil and garlic in a shallow glass or ceramic bowl and add the swordfish, turning to coat thoroughly. Cover with plastic film and leave to marinate for 15 minutes, turning once.
2 To make the salsa, combine all ingredients in a large bowl and mix well. Season with salt and pepper and set aside.
3 Remove the swordfish from the marinade and cook on a preheated chargrill over high heat for about 2 minutes on each side, turning once, until just cooked through.
4 Serve the fish with a spoonful of salsa and lime wedges if you like.

Serves 4

Mexican-style seafood pilaf

PREP **15 mins**   COOK **15–20 mins**   REST **10 mins**

I've included paella recipes in a couple of my previous books so I thought a pilaf that can be cooked on your barbie's wok burner might make a nice change. Essentially, the difference is that you cook a paella without a lid, and a perfect one should have a crispy base, while you cover a pilaf, to let the rice and seafood steam. Also, there's no smoked paprika in this recipe.

Choose any combination of three, four or five different types of seafood that you like.

You can also use white fish of your choice – try blue eye, ling or flathead.

2 tablespoons butter
2 tablespoons olive oil
3 cloves garlic, finely chopped
1 onion, finely chopped
2 jalapeno chillies, seeded and finely chopped
2 cups (400 g) medium or long-grain rice
1 × 400 g can diced tomatoes
1 teaspoon dried oregano
1 teaspoon sea salt
1.2 litres fish stock
400 g green king prawn meat
400 g boneless white fish cut into
   4 cm × 2 cm pieces
2 baby octopus, cleaned and quartered,
   or 1 calamari tube cut into rings
1 small raw blue swimmer crab, cleaned and
   cut into 4–6 pieces
8–12 mussels, beards removed
2 tablespoons coriander leaves, roughly chopped
1 tablespoon parsley leaves, roughly chopped
lemon wedges, to serve

1 Melt the butter in the oil in a shallow heavy-bottomed metal or clay pot over medium heat and add the garlic, onion, chillies and rice. Cook until the garlic and onion soften and the rice begins to colour.
2 Add the tomatoes, oregano and salt and cook for a couple of minutes over low heat, allowing the rice to absorb the flavour, then add the fish stock and the seafood, stirring well.
3 Bring to the boil then either place a lid on the pot or cover it tightly with foil and reduce to a simmer. Cook for 10 minutes over low heat or until rice is al dente. Turn off the heat and allow to rest for 10 minutes.
4 Serve straight from the pot, topped with coriander and parsley leaves, with lemon wedges.

Serves 4

Whole mackerel with green olive salad and colcannon

PREP 10 mins   COOK 25–30 mins

This is a hotchpotch that happily works. We don't cook enough delicious, oily fish and the sour and bitter flavours in the salad match it perfectly. Colcannon is a traditional Irish dish, made of mashed potatoes, cabbage and spring onions.

4 × whole mackerel, about 400 g each
2 tablespoons olive oil
sea salt and freshly ground black pepper, to taste

GREEN OLIVE SALAD
½ cup (70 g) slivered almonds
1 preserved lemon, flesh and seeds discarded,
  skin cut into 1 cm dice
8 large green Sicilian or other green olives,
  seeded and diced
1 teaspoon capers, rinsed and chopped
2 tablespoons flat-leaf parsley leaves, roughly chopped
2 tablespoons olive oil

COLCANNON
500 g desiree potatoes, peeled and roughly chopped
150 g savoy cabbage, finely sliced
¼ cup (60 ml) milk
100 g butter
½ teaspoon sea salt
4 spring onions, white and pale-green parts only,
  thinly sliced

1 To make the salad, lightly toast the almonds in a dry non-stick frying pan for a couple of minutes until browned. Allow to cool, then combine in a small bowl with lemon, olives, capers, parsley and olive oil. Set aside.

2 To make the colcannon, boil the potatoes in a saucepan with the salt and enough water to cover them. Cook with a lid on for about 15 minutes until nearly cooked, and then for a few minutes with the lid off to boil away most of the liquid. While the potatoes are boiling, cook cabbage in half of the butter in a small frying pan until soft. Drain potatoes well, then mash with the milk, butter and salt, stirring through the cabbage and spring onions. Set aside.

3 Brush the fish with the oil and season lightly with salt and pepper. Cook on a preheated flat grillplate over medium–high heat, turning once, until just cooked through. This should take about 10–15 minutes.

4 Serve the fish on individual plates, with a spoonful of the salad as a garnish and plenty of the colcannon.

Serves 4

Salmon fish cakes with tartare sauce and fennel and watercress salad

PREP 25 mins   COOK 20–25 mins

I'm always torn between salmon fish cakes and those made out of flaky white fish like blue eye. I can't get enough of either.

This all looks complicated, but it really isn't. You can make the tartare sauce well ahead of time and keep it in the fridge. Same with the fish and spuds; you can shape them into patties and just do the flour/egg/breadcrumb routine before you cook them.

FISH CAKES
400 g salmon, skin and bones removed
1 large (250–300 g) desiree potato, peeled
1 cup fresh breadcrumbs or 1½ cups of Japanese panko crumbs
¼ cup parsley, chopped
2 tablespoons finely grated parmesan
1 garlic clove, crushed
2 free-range or organic eggs, beaten
plenty of sea salt and white pepper
1 cup (150 g) plain flour
1 free-range or organic egg, beaten with a tablespoon of cold water
2 cups dry breadcrumbs
50 g butter
½ cup (125 ml) neutral oil

TARTARE SAUCE
1 cup (300 g) best-quality mayonnaise
2 tablespoons cornichons or dill pickles, finely chopped
1 tablespoons stuffed olives, chopped
1 tablespoon grated onion or golden shallot
1 tablespoon capers, chopped
1 tablespoon parsley, chopped
1 tablespoon lemon juice
pinch garlic powder

FENNEL AND WATERCRESS SALAD
3 tablespoons olive oil
1 tablespoon lemon juice
½ teaspoon Dijon mustard
1 bunch watercress, leaves picked, washed and dried
1 bulb fennel, core removed, very thinly sliced

1 To make the fish cakes, poach the salmon gently in salted water over low heat for about 10 minutes then drain well and flake with a fork. Boil the potato for 8–10 minutes until cooked, then mash with a fork and allow to cool.

2 Mix together the salmon, potato, fresh or panko breadcrumbs, parsley, parmesan, garlic, 2 beaten eggs, salt and pepper and shape carefully into neat patties. Chill for about 20 minutes until firm.

3 To crumb the fish cakes, take three shallow bowls. In one, place the seasoned flour; in the next, the beaten egg wash; and in the third, the breadcrumbs. Dip each fish cake in the flour, then the egg wash, and then immerse in the breadcrumbs. Melt the butter in the oil on a preheated flat grillplate over medium heat and fry the fish cakes until golden-brown.

4 To make the tartare sauce, combine all ingredients in a bowl and mix well. Store in an airtight container in the fridge until ready to serve.

5 To make the salad, mix together the oil, lemon juice and mustard in the base of a salad bowl then toss through the watercress and fennel, mixing well.

6 Place a couple of fish cakes on each plate and serve with a big dollop of tartare sauce and a spoonful of the salad.

Serves 4

Grilled snapper with turmeric and coriander butter

PREP 10 mins   COOK 6–8 mins

Another easy, yummy butter with heaps of flavour and, in this case, colour.

You can make flavoured butters and keep them in the fridge for a week or in the freezer for months, and use them to tart up any piece of fish or meat on the barbecue.

I've teamed the snapper with chargrilled asparagus just because it is such a great vegetable to grill on the barbie.

4 × 200–250 g pieces of snapper
2 bunches asparagus, woody ends removed
2 tablespoons olive oil

TURMERIC AND CORIANDER BUTTER
1 teaspoon coriander seeds
150 g butter, chopped into pieces and brought
   to room temperature
1 teaspoon ground turmeric
½ teaspoon tomato paste
1 tablespoon chives, finely chopped
sea salt and freshly ground black pepper, to taste

1 To make the butter, place the coriander seeds in a small frying pan over low heat and dry roast for about 2 minutes, then grind them in a mortar and pestle. (If you prefer, use 1 teaspoon of ground coriander instead.) Combine all ingredients in a food processor and blend until smooth, or else just place them all in a bowl and mash with the back of a fork.
2 Place a sheet of baking paper on your workbench, and put the butter in the centre. Use your hands to shape butter into a cylinder, then roll and twist the ends to make a bon bon. Refrigerate until ready to use.
3 Brush the fish and asparagus with the olive oil. Cook the fish on a preheated flat grillplate over medium–high heat for about 2–3 minutes on each side until it is just cooked through. At the same time, cook the asparagus on a preheated chargrill over high heat for about 3–4 minutes, turning occasionally.
4 Arrange the asparagus on four warmed plates and place the fish on top. Remove the flavoured butter from the fridge, gently unroll it and slice it into generous discs, then top each piece of fish with a disc.

Serves 4

Quick stew of mussels, cuttlefish and white beans >

PREP 10 mins   COOK 10 mins

If you can buy cleaned cuttlefish from your fishmonger, you'll be amazed how quickly you can whip up this really interesting, really filling one-pot wonder.

It's a great dish if the boys are over to watch the cricket or footy. I like to use Kinkawooka or Boston Bay mussels.

2 whole cuttlefish, cleaned (ask your fishmonger
   to do this) and cut into 1 cm dice
⅓ cup (80 ml) olive oil
50 g pancetta, diced
2 cloves garlic, crushed or finely chopped
1 onion, finely diced
½–1 red chilli, seeded and finely sliced
½ cup (125 ml) white wine
1 × 440 g can diced tomatoes
2 kg mussels, drained if in plastic pack
1 × 440 g can cannellini beans, drained and rinsed
handful of basil leaves, finely sliced
handful of flat-leaf parsley leaves, roughly chopped
freshly ground black pepper, to taste
crusty bread, to serve

1 Heat a large pot on your wok burner to very hot then add the cuttlefish and half the oil. Cook the cuttlefish for about 30 seconds until it is opaque, then remove it from the pot with a slotted spoon. Set aside.
2 Add pancetta to the pot and cook for about 1 minute. Add the remaining oil, garlic, onion and chilli and cook over high heat for about 1–2 minutes until the onion softens and the pancetta begins to colour. Add the white wine and tomatoes and cook for another 3–4 minutes.
3 Add the drained mussels and stir to coat well with the onion and tomato mixture. Place a lid on the pot and bring to the boil, shaking the pot occasionally. After about 2–3 minutes, when the mussels begin to open, fold the cannellini beans in gently so they don't break, then add reserved cuttlefish, basil, parsley and plenty of pepper.
4 Ladle into big bowls and serve with crusty bread.

Serves 4

SEAFOOD

Whole flounder with sauce vierge

PREP **15 mins**   COOK **approximately 10 mins**

White fish tastes so sweet and delicate when it's cooked on the bone, and flatter fish like flounder take no time at all to cook. John Dory also works well. You won't get a dozen of them for your mates on a standard barbie, but it makes a fabulous summer dinner for two, maybe four, depending on the size of the barbie.

**2 × whole flounder (ask your fishmonger
  to gut and scale them)**
sea salt and freshly ground black pepper
1 tablespoon butter
1 tablespoon olive oil
⅓ cup tarragon leaves
⅓ cup chives cut in 2 cm lengths
⅓ cup chervil leaves

SAUCE VIERGE
2 tomatoes, seeded and diced
85 ml extra virgin olive oil
25 ml lemon juice
1 teaspoon coriander seeds, crushed
8 basil leaves, finely sliced

1 To make the sauce vierge, prepare the tomatoes by making a little cross at the base of each with a sharp knife, then placing them in a saucepan of boiling water for 10–15 seconds. Transfer immediately to a large bowl of iced water for 30 seconds and then carefully remove the skins. Allow to cool then remove seeds and dice. Set aside.
2 Gently warm (but don't boil) the oil in a saucepan. Remove from the heat and add the lemon juice, coriander seeds, basil and tomato, stirring to combine. Reserve while you cook the fish.
3 Season fish with a little salt and pepper and melt the butter on a preheated flat grillplate. Brush the fish with oil then cook over medium–high heat, turning once, until just cooked through. This should take about 5 minutes on each side (check by putting the point of a sharp knife through the thickest part of the fish and sneaking a look).
4 Mix together the tarragon, chives and chervil.
5 Serve the fish on individual plates, spooning the sauce on top with a scattering of the herbs.

Serves 2

< Soy and white miso-marinated tuna

PREP 10 mins   MARINATE 4 hrs   COOK 2–4 mins

White miso paste is great in stir-fries and broths for chicken and fish dishes and also works as a marinade.

Mix it with a few other basic Japanese flavours and you've got something pretty special without much mucking around.

For something a bit different, you could also use this recipe to make fish kebabs.

4 × 150–200 g tuna steaks
2 bunches spring onions, white and pale-green
   parts only, sliced diagonally
2 tablespoons neutral oil
1 teaspoon white sesame seeds
1 teaspoon black sesame seeds

MISO MARINADE
½ cup (150 g) white miso paste
2 tablespoons mirin
2 tablespoons Japanese soy or light soy sauce
1½–2 cm piece ginger, peeled and grated
1 teaspoon sesame oil
1 tablespoon brown sugar
¼ cup (60 ml) water

1 Combine the marinade ingredients in a shallow glass or ceramic bowl and add the tuna steaks, turning to coat thoroughly. Cover with plastic film and leave in the fridge to marinate for 4 hours.
2 Bring the fish back to room temperature by removing from the fridge half an hour before cooking. Cook the tuna and the spring onions on a lightly oiled preheated chargrill over high heat for 1–2 minutes on each side, until the tuna is medium–rare, or until done to your liking.
3 Serve the tuna with the spring onions and sprinkled with the sesame seeds.

Serves 4

Spicy grilled Indian prawns

PREP 15 mins   MARINATE 2 hrs   COOK 5 mins

I'm struggling to think of a cuisine which doesn't work with prawns on the barbecue. This is pretty much Indian Spices 101, but that's no bad thing and you'll never make enough of these to satisfy the crowd. For what it's worth, they're great beer food.

12 large green (raw) king prawns
½ cup (125 ml) neutral oil
lemon wedges, to serve

MARINADE
2 tablespoons garam masala
1 tablespoon turmeric
1 teaspoon salt
½ teaspoon chilli powder
1 tablespoon paprika
1 teaspoon ground cumin
1 teaspoon ground cardamom
2 cloves garlic, crushed or grated
3–4 cm piece ginger, peeled and finely grated
2 tablespoons oil
lemon wedges, to serve

1 To prepare the prawns, twist off the head and carefully remove the shell. With a sharp knife, make a 5 mm-deep cut down the back, then remove the dark intestinal vein, leaving the last section of tail on.
2 Combine the marinade ingredients in a shallow glass or ceramic bowl and add the prawns, turning to coat thoroughly. Cover with plastic film and leave in the fridge to marinate for 2 hours.
3 Bring the prawns back to room temperature by removing from the fridge half an hour before cooking. Pour oil onto preheated flat grillplate and cook the prawns over medium–high heat for 2 minutes on each side.
4 Place prawns in a large bowl and serve with lemon wedges, finger bowls and plenty of cold beer.

Serves 2

Whole snapper with fennel and warm capsicum salsa

PREP **15 mins**   COOK **10–15 mins**

All you need for this is a barbie with a flat grillplate and a wok burner and the attention span to do two things at once.

You'll need about a quarter of an hour to chop the vegetables and fiddle with the fish, and a little more cooking time and you get a pretty flash result for very little effort.

2 × whole snapper or bream, about 350–400 g each
2 tablespoons olive oil
2 cloves garlic, crushed or very finely chopped
1 tablespoon fennel seeds, roughly chopped
**   or lightly crushed**
sea salt and freshly ground black pepper
50 ml Pernod (optional)
lemon or lime wedges, to serve (optional)

CAPSICUM SALSA
2 tablespoons olive oil
1 red onion, sliced
2 cloves garlic, crushed or very finely chopped
1 small fennel bulb, hard core removed, finely sliced,
**   wispy green fronds reserved and chopped**
1 red capsicum, white pith and seeds removed, diced
1 tomato, seeded and chopped

1 To make the salsa, heat the oil in a wok or large saucepan and cook the onion and garlic until soft. Add the sliced fennel and capsicum and cook over medium heat for about 5 minutes until capsicum is soft and fennel is golden-brown. Add the tomato and cook for about 5–8 minutes until it breaks down, then stir through the fennel fronds. Keep warm over low heat while you cook the fish.
2 Combine oil, garlic and the fennel seeds in a bowl with a little salt and pepper. Make three incisions into each side of the fish, and rub the mixture into the incisions.
3 Brush the fish with the oil and season lightly with salt and pepper. Cook on a preheated chargrill or flat grillplate over medium heat, turning once, until just cooked through. This should take about 10–15 minutes. Alternatively, cook fish in a metal fish holder over a medium charcoal or wood flame.
4 Transfer the fish to a large plate. If using Pernod, warm it in a small saucepan, tilt the pan and then ignite it with a match and pour it over the fish.
5 Serve the fish on individual plates, with the warm salsa and some lemon or lime wedges if you like.

Serves 2

< Scampi with lemon, black pepper and butter sauce

PREP 10 mins   COOK 20–25 mins

This is unashamedly for 'special'. Don't waste it on the in-laws or the neighbours who reciprocate with supermarket sausages.

It is a beautifully simple dish and, like most great food, it is all about the produce.

2–3 cups rock salt
8–12 scampi, halved lengthways

LEMON AND PEPPER SAUCE
150 g ghee (clarified butter) or butter
½ cup (125 ml) lemon juice
1 teaspoon freshly ground black pepper

1 Place the rock salt on a large tray in the middle of the barbecue with heat surrounding it on both sides, but not directly underneath. Close the hood and heat until the salt is very hot, for about 15 minutes.
2 To make the sauce, melt the ghee or butter in a saucepan over medium heat and add the lemon juice and pepper. Stir to combine and keep warm.
3 Place the scampi, flesh side up, on the salt-covered tray and bake in the middle of the barbecue with heat surrounding it on both sides, but not directly underneath, lid down, until the flesh just turns opaque. This should take about 5–10 minutes, depending on the heat of your barbecue.
4 Transfer the sauce to a bowl and serve the scampi on the tray in the middle of the table with finger bowls for messy fingers.

Serves 4 lucky people

Grilled salmon cutlets with herbs de Provence

PREP 5 mins   MARINATE 2 hrs   COOK 8–10 mins

There are times when dried herbs work better than fresh herbs, and this is one of them. The flavours of the dried herbs and lemon really enhance the richness of the salmon, which is extra-succulent, cooked on the bone as a cutlet.

You should be able to buy herbs de Provence, usually made up of dried marjoram, thyme, summer savory, basil, rosemary, fennel seeds and lavender, from specialty food shops.

4 × 250–300 g salmon cutlets
lemon wedges and lemon thyme leaves, to serve

HERB MARINADE
½ cup (125 ml) olive oil
zest and juice of one lemon
2 tablespoons herbs de Provence
2 cloves garlic, grated or crushed
½ teaspoon freshly ground black pepper

1 Combine the marinade ingredients in a shallow glass or ceramic bowl and add the fish, turning to coat thoroughly. Cover with plastic film and leave in the fridge to marinate for 2 hours, turning the fish after 1 hour.
2 Bring the salmon to room temperature by removing from the fridge half an hour before cooking.
3 Cook the fish on a preheated chargrill over medium–high heat for about 4–5 minutes on each side. Serve with lemon wedges and lemon thyme leaves.

Serves 4

Chilli lime trout

PREP 15 mins   COOK 10 mins   REST 5–10 mins

Wrapping fish in anything – foil, banana leaves, even wet newspaper, and cooking it on the barbie is a great way to keep it moist and to add all sorts of different flavours, from Asian to Italian to South American.

Here we add a few basic Mexican flavours to some trout, but you could use any smallish fresh or saltwater fish – like snapper or bream, for example.

1 tablespoon Worcestershire sauce
⅔ cup (160 ml) lime juice (juice of approximately 2 limes)
4 whole trout (approximately 400–450 g each)
⅓ cup (80 ml) olive oil
1 small red onion, sliced into rings
4 roma tomatoes, sliced
sea salt and freshly ground black pepper, to taste
2 jalapeno chillies, seeded and sliced
1 lime, sliced
leaves from about 20 fresh oregano sprigs or
  1 teaspoon dried oregano
50 g butter

1 Combine the Worcestershire sauce and lime juice in a small jug and set aside.
2 Cut four pieces of foil, big enough to wrap each fish completely, and rub one side of each with oil.
3 Place half of the onion rings and half of the tomato slices on the pieces of foil, with a piece of fish on top of each. Season well with salt and pepper, then add chillies, lime slices, oregano leaves and the rest of the onion and tomato. Cut the butter into eight pieces and place two pieces on each piece of fish. Pour over the lime juice and Worcestershire sauce mix and wrap the fish into four tight parcels.
4 Cook on a preheated chargrill or flat grillplate over medium heat for about 10 minutes, then rest for about 5–10 minutes before serving.

Serves 4

Ling and salmon skewers with dill mayonnaise >

PREP 10 mins   COOK 4–5 mins

You can really use any firm white fish here, and take your pick from salmon or ocean trout. I'd be just as happy with blue eye and ocean trout, as long as you end up with the pink and white effect.

The Dill Mayo is delicious with this but the Lime Mayo on page 58 would also work well. Or you could cheat and use good-quality store-bought mayonnaise and flavour it with dill and lemon.

400 g thick ling fillet, skin and bones removed
400 g salmon fillet, skin and bones removed
sea salt and freshly ground black pepper, to taste
2 tablespoons neutral oil
steamed asparagus, to serve

DILL MAYONNAISE
2 free-range or organic egg yolks
1 teaspoon Dijon mustard
150 ml extra virgin olive oil
100 ml peanut oil
2 tablespoons dill, finely chopped
finely grated zest from one lemon

1 To make the dill mayonnaise, place the egg yolks and Dijon mustard in a large bowl. Add the oils in the thinnest possible stream, whisking vigorously with a wire whisk or fork until the mixture thickens. Gently fold through the dill and lemon zest and refrigerate until ready to use.
2 Cut the ling and salmon fillets into 3–4 cm pieces. Place the fish pieces on skewers, alternating between ling and salmon. Season with a little salt and pepper.
3 Cook on a lightly oiled preheated flat grillplate over medium–high heat for about 4–5 minutes, turning occasionally.
4 Serve the fish skewers with a dollop of the mayonnaise and some asparagus.

Serves 4 as a light meal

Tabbouleh

PREP 15–20 mins

You can pick a fight about the correct spelling of this, but there's no blueing about the wonderful clean flavours and how well tabbouleh sits with rich, fatty meat. It's perfect with the Chermoula-crusted Leg of Lamb (see recipe on page 100) or any other roasted leg or shoulder.

2 tablespoons fine bulgur
2 bunches flat-leaf parsley, thick stems discarded,
 leaves very finely chopped
handful mint, leaves very finely chopped
1 tomato, seeded and finely diced
½ small cucumber, peeled, seeded and finely diced
2 tablespoons lemon juice
sea salt and freshly ground black pepper

1 Soak the bulgur in ½ cup boiling water for 10 minutes, then drain and rinse under cold water in a colander or sieve. Set aside to cool.
2 Combine all ingredients in a large salad bowl, mixing well, and season with salt and pepper.

Serves 4

Bacon and egg potato salad >

PREP 10 mins   COOK 20 mins

So, what could make potato salad even better?
   (Homer Simpson voice inside your head please) Baaacon.
   You do need a few sour or bitter flavours to balance everything else evil going on here. Just try to stop going back to the fridge for leftovers – if there are any.

750 g new potatoes (unpeeled) or kipflers (peeled)
4 free-range or organic eggs
2 rashers thick, rindless bacon, cut into 1 cm pieces
4 cornichons, sliced
½ stick celery, finely sliced
1 bunch chives, finely chopped
1 cup (300 g) best-quality mayonnaise
sea salt and freshly ground black pepper, to taste

1 Steam or boil the potatoes for 8–10 minutes or until tender. Drain immediately and allow to cool, then cut into 2 cm chunks.
2 Put the eggs in cold water in a saucepan, bring to the boil, then simmer for 5 minutes. Rinse immediately under cold water. Once the eggs have cooled, peel and quarter them.
3 Fry bacon in a small frying pan over medium heat for a couple of minutes until slightly crisp, then drain on paper towel.
4 Gently combine the potatoes, eggs, bacon, cornichons, celery, most of the chives and mayonnaise in a large salad bowl, sprinkle over the rest of the chives, and season with salt and pepper.

Serves 4–6

Radicchio with fennel and walnuts

PREP 10 mins

Nice little combination of flavours here that could be served as a starter, especially with some interesting cheese – like maybe manchego – added. Mind you, it's just fine the way it is, and complements chicken and fish particularly well.

1 head radicchio, washed and finely sliced
1 small fennel bulb, hard core removed, finely sliced
½ cup flat-leaf parsley, roughly chopped
1 cup (120 g) walnut halves

DRESSING
⅓ cup (80 ml) walnut oil
2 tablespoons lemon juice

1 To make the dressing, mix together the walnut oil and lemon juice in a large salad bowl.
2 Gently toss through the radicchio, fennel, flat-leaf parsley and walnut halves, mixing well. Serve immediately.

Serves 4

Strozzapreti with zucchini and cherry tomatoes

PREP 15 mins   COOK 15–20 mins

Something filling to put on the table. You can use any sort of short pasta but the strozzapreti has an interesting shape and an interesting name – it means 'priest choker' – and you can match it with all sorts of vegetables. I like to include the onion and tomato for their sweetness, but after that it's a pretty moveable feast: broccoli, asparagus, baby spinach or cavolo nero would all be good.

400 g strozzapreti pasta
⅓ cup (80 ml) olive oil
1 red onion, sliced
2 cloves garlic, sliced
2–3 zucchini, cut into 6 cm × 1 cm batons
250 g cherry tomatoes, halved
handful flat-leaf parsley, roughly chopped
sea salt and freshly ground black pepper, to taste

DRESSING
½ cup (125 ml) extra virgin olive oil
2 tablespoons red-wine vinegar

1 Bring a large saucepan of salted water to the boil then add the strozzapreti and simmer, uncovered, for about 10 minutes or until al dente. Drain and rinse under cold water in a colander or sieve, then drain again and set aside to cool.
2 While the pasta is cooking, heat half the ordinary olive oil in a heavy frying pan and cook the onion and garlic over low–medium heat until soft. Transfer onion and garlic to a bowl and set aside to cool.
3 Add the other half of the ordinary olive oil to the frying pan and fry the zucchini over high heat for about 2–3 minutes until brown. If you prefer, you could fry the zucchini on a preheated flat grillplate over high heat for about 2–3 minutes. Set aside to cool.
4 To make the dressing, mix together the extra virgin olive oil and vinegar in a large salad bowl, then toss through all the other ingredients, mixing well. Season well with salt and pepper.

Serves 6

Pear, rocket and gorgonzola salad

PREP 10 mins

Pears and gorgonzola are just so delicious together, and even better with some peppery young rocket leaves in the mix.

There's dolce (sweet) gorgonzola and piccante (sharp) gorgonzola; you can use either, but I prefer the rich sweetness of the dolce. You could always add some crispy bacon or pancetta to this just before serving.

200 g baby rocket leaves, washed and dried
2 packham or beurre bosc pears, cored and sliced
150 g gorgonzola, cut into 2–3 cm pieces

DRESSING
⅓ cup (80 ml) extra virgin olive oil
2 tablespoons white-wine vinegar
sea salt and freshly ground black pepper, to taste

1 To make the dressing, mix together all the ingredients in a large salad bowl.
2 Toss through the rocket leaves and pear slices, mixing well. Scatter the gorgonzola over the top and serve immediately.

Serves 4

Cajun-style rice salad

PREP 10 mins   COOK 10 mins

If the basics of the French mirepoix are onions, celery and carrots, in New Orleans, they're onions, celery and green capsicum.

I've simply thrown those flavours into a rice salad; you could add some tomato and corn if you wanted to, but I'd rather keep it simple.

1½ cups long-grain rice
1 red onion, finely diced
2 sticks celery, sliced
1 green capsicum, white insides and seeds removed, cut into 1 cm dice
½ teaspoon dried thyme leaves
handful of flat-leaf parsley leaves, roughly chopped
sea salt and freshly ground black pepper, to taste

DRESSING
3 tablespoons neutral oil
3 tablespoons white-wine vinegar
1 teaspoon Tabasco sauce (optional)

1 Bring a large saucepan of salted water to the boil then add the rice and simmer, uncovered, for about 10 minutes or until cooked. Drain and rinse under cold water in a colander or sieve, and set aside to cool.
2 To make the dressing, mix together all the ingredients in a small jug or bowl.
3 Combine the cooked rice and the rest of the ingredients in a large salad bowl, stir the dressing through and season well with salt and pepper. Serve immediately.

Serves 4–6

SALAD & VEG

Stir-fried brussels sprouts with pancetta

PREP 10 mins   COOK 15–20 mins

I know, I know, you hate brussels sprouts and would never let them ruin a good barbecue.

Well, you haven't tried these brussels sprouts with lots of great flavours that aren't trying to hide the flavour of the sprouts, but enhance them.

Come on, be brave and give them a try.

2 tablespoons olive oil
50 g pancetta in a single thick slice,
   chopped into 1 cm pieces
2 cloves garlic, crushed or chopped
¼–½ teaspoon chilli flakes
300 g brussels sprouts, halved if large
2 tablespoons water or white wine, for cooking
1 teaspoon sugar
1 tablespoon white-wine vinegar
handful baby spinach leaves
1 cup (140 g) pecans
sea salt and freshly ground black pepper, to taste

1 Heat the olive oil in a heavy frying pan and add the pancetta pieces, cooking over medium heat until it begins to crisp.
2 Add the garlic, chilli flakes and brussels sprouts and toss to combine. Add a couple of tablespoons of water or white wine to the pan and reduce heat to a simmer, cooking sprouts for about 10 minutes until al dente, adding more liquid if needed. Sprinkle over the sugar and stir well, then add the vinegar, cooking for another minute before stirring through the baby spinach and pecans.
3 Finish with some pepper and check taste for salt – it shouldn't need it with the salty pancetta, but add a little if you think you need to. Works very nicely with a plain grilled steak.

Serves 4

SALAD & VEG

< Red and white witlof salad with ranch dressing

PREP 15 mins   COOK 5 mins

Americans love their ranch dressing. Truth is, they love anything with mayonnaise in it.

Ranch dressing is sometimes a dip for crudites and sometimes a salad dressing, though it would absolutely swamp a green salad.

I suggest that you make this a first course before something meaty and substantial and keep adding more of your favourite raw vegetables. I used broccoli, beans, peas and asparagus, but you could just as easily try carrots, celery, red or yellow capsicum, cucumber or zucchini.

1 red witlof, core discarded, leaves washed and dried
1 white witlof, core discarded, leaves washed and dried
2–3 cups seasonal vegetables, cut into bite-sized pieces

RANCH DRESSING
½ cup (150 g) best-quality mayonnaise
½ cup (125 ml) buttermilk
¼ cup (60 g) sour cream
1 tablespoon lemon juice
1 tablespoon white-wine vinegar
1 clove garlic, crushed or grated
1 tablespoon flat-leaf parsley, finely chopped
1 tablespoon chives, finely chopped
sea salt and freshly ground black pepper, to taste

1 To make the dressing, combine all ingredients in a small bowl and mix well. Season well with salt and pepper then store, covered with plastic wrap, in the fridge until ready to use.
2 Blanch the seasonal vegetables in boiling water for a couple of minutes, then quickly refresh them in iced water and then drain.
3 Arrange witlof and vegetables on a large serving plate and drizzle the dressing over the top. Serve immediately.

Serves 4 or more

Roast balsamic red onions and treviso with thyme

PREP 10 mins   COOK approximately 30 mins

Nothing too complicated here, just the sweetness of the onions and balsamic, matched with the splendid bitterness of the treviso. If you can't get treviso, radicchio will do just as well.

This is a lovely wintery dish to have alongside a butterflied leg of lamb or a whole roast one.

⅓ cup (80 ml) olive oil
4 red onions, peeled and quartered
1 large or 2 medium treviso, quartered, leaves washed and dried
1 tablespoon fresh thyme leaves
sea salt and freshly ground black pepper, to taste
⅔ cup (160 ml) balsamic vinegar

1 Close the lid of your barbecue then preheat it to very hot.
2 Place the oil in the bottom of a baking dish and place the onions in, cut-side down, arranging the treviso in the dish beside them. Sprinkle with thyme leaves and plenty of salt and pepper, then pour the balsamic over the top.
3 Place the baking dish in the middle of the barbecue with heat surrounding it on both sides, but not directly underneath, and the hood down. Cook for about half an hour until the onions are soft and they and the treviso have absorbed some of the balsamic.

Serves 4

SALAD & VEG

Piquant potato salad

PREP 10 mins   COOK 8–10 mins

Here's one for the grown-ups, or at least grown-ups with grown-up tastes. It is the opposite of an American-style salad with sweet ingredients and a sugary dressing.

Serve with a steak or grilled fish.

500 g kipfler potatoes, peeled
6 cornichons, sliced
1 tablespoon capers, rinsed and chopped
1 stalk celery, sliced
½ red onion, finely sliced

DRESSING
1½ tablespoons grain mustard
½ cup (150 g) best-quality mayonnaise
1 tablespoon white-wine vinegar
2 tablespoons dill leaves, chopped
sea salt and freshly ground black pepper, to taste

1 Steam or boil the potatoes for 8–10 minutes or until tender. Drain immediately and allow to cool, then cut into 2 cm slices.
2 To make the dressing, combine all ingredients in a small jug or bowl, stirring well to combine.
3 Place the potato, cornichons, capers, celery and onion in a large salad bowl, and gently stir the dressing through, mixing well. Serve immediately, or cover with plastic wrap and refrigerate, bringing back to room temperature before serving.

Serves 4–6

Fusilli and bocconcini salad with pesto sauce >

PREP 15 mins   COOK 10–15 mins

This is an easy way to fill up a crowd, and fusilli are great because the sauce gets stuck in all those little swirls, so you get more of it.

Of course, once you've got the knack of throwing together a pesto sauce, you can use it in lots of pasta dishes, on meat or seafood or in salads.

500 g fusilli pasta
2 tablespoons olive oil
200 g baby bocconcini, sliced
250 g cherry or grape tomatoes, halved

PESTO
½ cup (80 g) pine nuts
2 cloves garlic, chopped or crushed
1 bunch of basil, leaves picked
50 g freshly grated parmesan cheese
½ cup (125 ml) olive oil
sea salt and freshly ground black pepper, to taste

1 Bring a large saucepan of salted water to the boil, then add pasta and cook according to the instructions on the pack until al dente. Drain and rinse under cold water in a colander or sieve, then transfer to a large serving bowl. Drizzle the olive oil over the pasta and stir through to prevent it sticking, then set aside to cool.
2 To make the pesto, lightly toast the pine nuts in a dry non-stick frying pan over high heat for a couple of minutes, watching closely so that they don't burn, until they are golden-brown. Allow to cool, then place the pine nuts, garlic, basil leaves and parmesan in a food processor and pulse until a coarse paste forms. Slowly add the oil in a stream through the funnel, still pulsing, until the mixture has the consistency of a thick sauce. Season with salt and pepper to taste.
3 Stir the pesto, bocconcini and cherry tomatoes through the pasta and serve immediately, or cover with plastic wrap and refrigerate, bringing back to room temperature before serving.

Serves 6–10

Spicy potato bake

PREP 10 mins   COOK 30–40 mins

Something a bit different that you may have to throw in the oven if the barbie lid has to be up so that everything else can cook.

Good, big flavours to go with steaks, bangers and all sorts of red meat dishes.

⅓ cup (80 ml) olive oil
2 onions, finely sliced
4 cloves garlic, finely sliced
2 tablespoons ground cumin
½ tablespoon ground paprika (not smoked)
½ teaspoon cayenne pepper, more or less to taste
handful of flat-leaf parsley, roughly chopped
sea salt and freshly ground black pepper, to taste
400 g can diced tomatoes
1 cup (250 ml) chicken stock
1 kg desiree potatoes

1 Preheat your barbecue to very hot.
2 Heat half the oil in a large heavy-based baking dish and cook the onions and garlic over medium heat until golden. Add the cumin, paprika, cayenne, parsley, salt and pepper to the dish and stir well to combine. Add the tomatoes and stock and stir again.
3 Chop potatoes into 2–3 cm dice and place them in a large bowl. Drizzle remaining oil and sprinkle extra salt over them, and toss until they are well coated. Add the potatoes to the tomato mixture and place the baking dish in the middle of the barbecue with heat surrounding it on both sides, but not directly underneath. Close the hood and cook for half an hour or so, until the tops of the spuds are crispy and they are cooked through and soft when skewered. Add a little more stock or water if the mixture starts to dry out.

Serves 6–8

Smothered corn >

PREP 10 mins   COOK 40–45 mins

This is a delicious way to cook corn. It's better with fresh corn cut off the cob, when it's in season, but I won't tell anyone if you use frozen. The purists wouldn't have red capsicum in there either.

6 corn cobs or 4 cups (640 g) frozen corn kernels
⅓ cup (80 ml) neutral oil
1 onion, finely diced
2 cloves garlic, finely diced
1 tomato, seeded and finely diced
½ red capsicum, white insides and seeds removed, cut into 1 cm dice
¼–½ teaspoon cayenne pepper
sea salt and freshly ground black pepper, to taste
1 tablespoon fresh thyme leaves

1 If using fresh corn, bring a large saucepan of water to the boil, add the corn and cook, covered, for 10–15 minutes or until the corn is tender. Gently remove the corn from the pot and transfer to a plate. Once cool enough to handle, stand each corn cob up on a chopping board and carefully slice the kernels off with a large knife. Set aside the kernels.
2 Heat the oil in a heavy frying pan and cook the onion and garlic over low–medium heat until soft. Add the tomato and capsicum and cook for about 3–5 minutes until the capsicum softens slightly. Add the corn kernels, cayenne, salt and lots of pepper and cook, stirring occasionally until the corn is tender. This should take about 20 minutes.
3 Stir through the thyme leaves and cook for another minute or two. Check seasoning and serve with any barbecued meat.

Serves 4–6

SALAD & VEG

Frisee, blue cheese, bacon and hazelnut salad

PREP 10 mins   COOK 2–5 mins

More a shopping list than a recipe, there's not a lot of cooking to do here. Some flavours just go so well together. For me, this is much more of a starter-type of salad than something to lob on your plate beside a steak.

1 frisee lettuce, leaves washed and dried, tough outer leaves discarded
2 rashers thick, rindless bacon or pancetta, cut into 3 cm pieces
⅔ cup (100 g) hazelnuts
½ bunch chives, finely chopped
150–200 g blue cheese, such as gorgonzola, stilton or roquefort

DRESSING
½ cup (125 ml) hazelnut oil
¼ cup (60 ml) white-wine vinegar
sea salt and freshly ground black pepper, to taste

1 Fry bacon in a small frying pan over medium heat for a couple of minutes until slightly crisp, then drain on paper towel.
2 To make the dressing, mix together all the ingredients in a large salad bowl. Toss through the lettuce leaves, bacon, hazelnuts and chives, mixing well. Arrange on serving plates and crumble cheese over the top.

Serves 4

Watermelon salad >

PREP 10 mins

This is all about contrasting flavours and textures: sweet, crisp watermelon; salty, squishy olives; crumbly feta and as much chilli bite as you can handle.

500 g watermelon (skin removed), cut roughly into 3–5 cm pieces
100–200 g feta cheese
10 pitted kalamata olives
about 20 mint leaves
1 teaspoon chilli powder
freshly ground black pepper, to taste

DRESSING
juice of 1 lime
2 tablespoons extra virgin olive oil

1 To make dressing, mix lime juice and oil together in a small jug.
2 To make salad, combine watermelon, feta, olives and mint leaves in a large salad bowl. Drizzle dressing over salad, and sprinkle chilli and pepper on top.

Serves 4–6

Roasted winter vegetables

PREP **15 mins**   COOK **approximately 30 mins**

The trick to baking root vegetables for a 'fast and easy' cookbook is to cut them nice and small so they will cook quickly.

I like to mix up spuds, carrots and parsnips and throw in some onion or leek for sweetness, and maybe some whole unpeeled garlic cloves for flavour. Lots of olive oil and plenty of sea salt and you're away.

I love the way you get a different vegetable flavour and texture with every bite in this recipe. Don't feel obliged to include every vegetable listed here; please use it more as a guide.

2 desiree potatoes
1 small celeriac
4–6 Jerusalem artichokes
2 carrots
2 parsnips
1 fennel bulb, hard core removed
2 leeks, white and pale green parts only
4–8 baby golden or traditional beetroot,
**   scrubbed but not peeled**
⅔ cup (160 ml) olive oil
8 garlic cloves, unpeeled
6 sprigs thyme
4 fresh bay leaves
sea salt, to taste

1 Peel and cut the potatoes, celeriac, artichokes, carrots and parsnips into even-sized pieces. Cut the fennel into slices, and the leeks in half lengthways. Put the oil in a large, non-stick baking dish and add the chopped vegetables and beetroot, garlic, thyme and bay leaves. Toss to coat and sprinkle salt over the top.
2 Place the baking dish in the middle of a very hot, preheated barbecue with heat surrounding it on both sides, but not directly underneath, and bake for about half an hour, with the hood down, until vegetables soften and begin to brown. Serve with any barbecued meat.

Serves 4–6 comfortably

SALAD & VEG

Corny coleslaw

PREP 10 mins   COOK 10–15 mins

Corn gives coleslaw a nice sweetness that needs to be balanced with some vinegar in this barbecue classic. There's nothing wrong with the cabbage/onion/carrot/celery/mayo basic, or a more European version with lots of grain mustard through it, but it is nice to have a change. See the photograph on page 127.

3 corn cobs or 400 g frozen corn kernels, thawed
¼ white cabbage (thick white stems removed), finely sliced
¼ red cabbage (thick white stems removed), finely sliced
1 red onion, finely sliced
1 green capsicum, white pith and seeds removed,
** cut into 1 cm dice**
1 stalk celery, sliced
handful of flat-leaf parsley leaves, roughly chopped
sea salt and freshly ground black pepper, to taste

DRESSING
⅔ cup (200 g) best-quality mayonnaise
1 tablespoon white-wine vinegar

1 If you are using whole corn cobs, bring a large saucepan of water to the boil, add the corn and cook, covered, for 10–15 minutes or until the corn is tender. Gently remove the corn from the pot and transfer to a plate. Once cool enough to handle, stand each corn cob up on a chopping board and carefully slice the kernels off with a large knife. Allow kernels to cool.
2 To make the dressing, mix together the mayonnaise and vinegar in a large salad bowl. Toss through the rest of the ingredients, mixing well. Season well with salt and pepper, adding more mayo if the coleslaw is too dry. Taste and add more vinegar if necessary.
3 Cover the coleslaw and chill in the fridge for half an hour before serving.

Serves lots

Corn on the cob with flavoured butter >

PREP 5 mins   COOK 10–15 mins

Corn stripped of its husk and thrown on the barbie is simply delicious, especially as the kernels begin to caramelise and almost blacken.

The other thing you can do with corn is to cook it with one of the flavoured butters in this book, like the Salsa Verde Butter on page 81, Maitre d' hotel Butter on page 82, Maple Butter on page 126, Herb Butter on page 139 or the Turmeric and Coriander Butter on page 150. Pull the husks back up to seal in the moisture and half-steam, half-barbecue the corn.

4–6 corn cobs
4–6 tablespoons (80–120 g) softened butter
sea salt and freshly ground black pepper, to taste

1 To make corn on the cob with ordinary butter, strip the corn of their husks, smear with a generous amount of butter, and cook on a preheated chargrill or flat grillplate over medium heat for about 10–15 minutes, turning regularly.
2 To make corn on the cob with one of the flavoured butters or sauces, peel back the husk, discard those annoying pale filaments, and smear the corn with a generous amount of flavoured butter. Season well with salt and pepper, pull the husks back up and twist the tops.
3 Let the corn half-steam and half-cook on a preheated chargrill over medium heat for about 10–15 minutes, turning regularly, allowing all the wonderful flavoured butters to permeate the kernels. Yum!

Serves 4–6

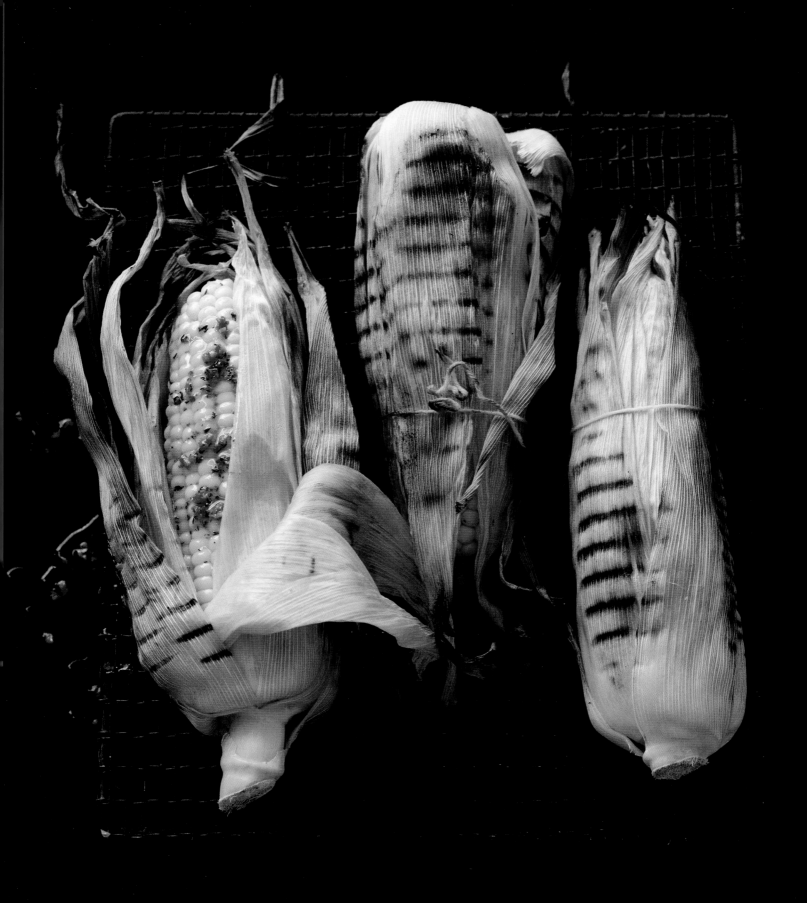

Hazelnut panettone toasted sandwiches

PREP **10 mins**   COOK **5 mins**

As a parent, it's fair to say that I'm no fan of Nutella. It's full of sugar and the ads describing it as good for kids' energy levels are just plain offensive.

But it can play a role as a once-in-a-while treat for dessert (just don't spread it on sandwiches for the school day lunch box).

I like to make these with leftover panettone, but you could easily use brioche. You can also decide whether to include the hazelnuts; they're even more child-friendly without.

8 slices panettone
enough soft butter to butter lightly – about 50 g
Nutella, to taste
16–20 marshmallows, halved
12 unsalted hazelnuts, lightly crushed (optional)

1 Butter one side of the panettone slices, and spread the inside of four slices quite thickly with Nutella. Place the halved marshmallows evenly over the Nutella and sprinkle over the crushed hazelnuts if using. Top with the other slices of panettone, buttered side out.
2 Cook on a preheated flat grillplate over medium heat for a couple of minutes each side until the marshmallows have melted and the panettone is golden-brown.

Serves 4

Toasted brioche with red berries and caramel sauce >

PREP **10 mins**   COOK **8–10 mins**

There's not much cooking to this, just the caramel sauce (which everyone loves) and toasting some brioche slices on the chargrill.

Still, it makes for a delicious dessert which is so, so easy, in summer when berries are at their best and cheapest.

4 slices brioche
4 scoops vanilla ice-cream, to serve
2 cups mixed red berries like strawberries,
** raspberries, redcurrants**

CARAMEL SAUCE
⅔ cup sugar
2 tablespoons water
1 cup (250 ml) cream

1 To make the sauce, dissolve the sugar in water in a small, non-stick saucepan over high heat for about 3–5 minutes. When it becomes a medium caramel colour, add the cream, a little at a time, stirring constantly. When the sauce starts to boil, remove it from the heat before it boils over and keep stirring for about a minute until it is smooth.
2 Toast the brioche slices on a preheated chargrill over high heat for a minute or two on each side. Remove from heat, place on plates and top with a scoop of ice-cream and some berries, and then pour over the caramel sauce.

Serves 4

DESSERT

Tiramisu and raspberry parfait

PREP 20 mins

Tiramisu and Croissant Bread and Butter Pud are the two most-prepared desserts at my dining table. They appeared in *The Great Aussie Bloke's Cookbook* and *The Great Aussie Family Cookbook* respectively.

Here's a tiramisu with a bit of a twist, matched with raspberries and served in individual parfait glasses.

4 free-range or organic eggs, separated
125 g icing sugar, sifted
1 cup (250 g) mascarpone cheese
50 ml brandy or marsala
400 ml strong black coffee
200–225 g sponge finger biscuits
125 g raspberries
50 g good-quality dark chocolate

1 Put the egg yolks and icing sugar into the bowl of an electric mixer and beat on medium speed until the mixture thickens and turns pale yellow, then fold through the mascarpone on low speed. Transfer to large bowl and set aside.
2 Clean and dry the bowl of the electric mixer, put in the eggwhites and beat on high speed until stiff, then fold the beaten eggwhites into the mascarpone mixture.
3 Place a spoonful of the mixture in the bottom of four to six parfait glasses, depending on their size (you might finally get to use the ones your grandma left you).
4 In a large bowl combine the brandy or marsala with the coffee, then dip the sponge biscuits into this mixture and place half of them on top of the mascarpone mixture, dividing them equally between four glasses.
5 Add another spoonful of the mascarpone mixture to each parfait glass, then a layer of raspberries, a little more of the mascarpone mixture, more soaked sponge fingers, and then mascarpone, raspberries and, finally, mascarpone again on top.
6 Use a vegetable peeler to shave the chocolate and sprinkle the shavings on top of each parfait. Refrigerate until ready to serve, but for at least 1 hour.

Serves 4–6

< Boozy barbecue fruit parcels

PREP **15 mins**   COOK **approximately 5 mins**

You can choose your favourite tipple for these very straightforward little fruit desserts.

Rum and scotch work nicely, but the daggy sweeter drops are even better: think Cointreau, Grand Marnier or even Frangelico. I'd dodge the creamy ones like Baileys or Kahlua.

Use whatever fruits are in season, such as strawberries, bananas, pineapples, orange or mandarin segments, kiwifruit, mangoes, pitted cherries or peaches. I like to use passionfruit pulp as well.

4 cups mixed seasonal fruit cut into bite-sized pieces
4 teaspoons brown sugar
2 teaspoons butter
⅓ cup (80 g) Cointreau (or other as above)
1 teaspoon finely grated orange zest
cream or vanilla ice-cream, to serve

1 Cut four pieces of foil and four pieces of baking paper into squares of about 20 cm each, and place them on top of each other to create four squares of double thickness.
2 Place each of the double squares into a shallow bowl (this makes them easier to fill) and divide the fruit between them. Top each with a teaspoon of brown sugar, a bit of butter, a slosh of booze and a pinch of orange zest, then join the four corners, twisting to make them airtight.
3 Cook on a preheated flat grillplate over high heat for about 5 minutes, then remove each parcel from the barbecue and place it back in a bowl. Serve unopened so the sweet, fruity, boozy aroma can be enjoyed at the table.
4 Serve with cream or ice-cream.

Serves 4

Grilled pineapple and strawberries with butterscotch sauce

PREP **10 mins**   COOK **8–10 mins**

Make the skewers and the sauce early in the day, and quickly heat the sauce while you grill the fruit. Desserts don't get much easier.

½ pineapple
12 strawberries
vanilla ice-cream, to serve (optional)

BUTTERSCOTCH SAUCE
½ cup (110 g) brown sugar
1 teaspoon water
300 ml pouring cream

1 Peel the pineapple, then cut into 3 cm pieces, discarding core. Thread the pineapple pieces and strawberries onto four skewers and refrigerate until ready to use.
2 To make the sauce, melt the brown sugar with a teaspoon of water in a small, non-stick saucepan over high heat for about 3–5 minutes. When it becomes a medium caramel colour, add the cream, a little at a time, stirring constantly. When the sauce starts to boil, remove it from the heat before it boils over and keep stirring for about a minute until it is smooth.
3 Remove the skewers from the fridge and place them on a preheated lightly oiled chargrill over high heat. Cook for just a few minutes on each side, turning once.
4 Remove the skewers from the heat and place one on each plate. Drizzle the butterscotch sauce over skewers and serve with a scoop of ice-cream, if you like.

Serves 4

DESSERT

189

Panettone french toast

PREP 10 mins   COOK 8–10 mins

Panettone can be a bit like the yellow socks or orange and green striped tie that you get for Christmas – 'Gee, thanks Gran, I'll put it in the drawer with last year's'. I reckon that for every great, moist, spice and citrus-redolent baked wonder, I've had ten dry bland things that aren't as interesting as commercial fruit loaf.

So, what to do with a dud panettone? Slather it in eggs, butter and maple syrup and make a French toast dessert out of it.

2 free-range or organic eggs
2 tablespoons thickened cream
1 teaspoon vanilla extract
50 g butter (plus extra for frying)
4 slices panettone, 1 cm thick
maple syrup, to serve
vanilla ice-cream, to serve (optional)

1 Mix the eggs, cream and vanilla together in a shallow bowl. Melt the butter on a preheated flat grillplate over very high heat. As you cook, you may need to add some more.
2 Working very quickly, immerse each piece of panettone in the egg-and-cream mixture and place it on the barbecue immediately, turning when golden-brown (dithering with the panettone in the mixture can lead to dissolved panettone – very dull).
3 To serve, place one piece of French toast panettone on each plate and pour over plenty of maple syrup and maybe some ice-cream for the kids.

Serves 4

Bananas Foster >

PREP 5 mins   COOK 5–8 mins

Bananas Foster and Bread Pudding are the two traditional, signature desserts from New Orleans. It's a town that I've only been to a couple of times but it is one of my favourites in the world.

The original recipe is from the wonderful old Brennan's Restaurant, one of so many great places to eat there.

⅓ cup (80 g) unsalted butter
1 cup (200 g) brown sugar
½ tablespoon cinnamon
⅓ cup (80 ml) banana liqueur
4 bananas, peeled and halved lengthways
½ cup (125 ml) dark rum
4 scoops vanilla ice-cream

1 Melt the butter in a frying pan over high heat, then add the brown sugar, cinnamon and banana liqueur, stirring to combine. Add the bananas, stirring gently, and cook until they soften. Add the rum and heat through quickly, then tip the frying pan to one side and ignite the liquid with a match.
2 To serve, place a scoop of ice-cream in each dessert bowl and arrange four banana pieces on top, spooning the sauce over the top.

Serves 4

DESSERT

Five minute blueberry cheesecake trifle

PREP **10 mins**   COOK **5 mins**

Set your mind to it and you really could make this in 5 minutes. Take it easy and give yourself 10. It's nice to be able to serve dessert without spending the day worrying about it. Having said that, you'll be surprised just how good it is for so little effort.

2 tablespoons slivered almonds
100 g amaretti biscuits
1 cup (250 g) mascarpone
250 g packet cream cheese
2 tablespoons sugar
125 g blueberries
2 tablespoons sweet marsala

1 To toast the almonds, place them in a dry frying pan over medium heat and shake them regularly until they brown. Allow to cool and set aside.
2 Place the amaretti biscuits in a food processor and blend to make coarse crumbs. Place amaretti crumbs into base of four parfait or ordinary glasses, reserving a small amount of crumbs.
3 Combine the mascarpone and cream cheese with one tablespoon of the sugar in the bowl of an electric mixer and mix well, then spoon the mixture into the glasses.
4 Place half the blueberries, marsala and remaining sugar in a food processor and blend to a sauce consistency.
5 Spoon the blueberry marsala sauce over the top and top with the remaining blueberries, amaretti crumbs and toasted almonds. Serve immediately.

Serves 4

DESSERT

< Chargrilled pears with cheddar cheese and sultana chutney

PREP **15 mins** COOK **30 mins**

If, like me, you don't have a sweet tooth, then here's something that is easy, different and will soak up the red wine.

You can choose a good English cheddar or my local favourite, the Pyengana from Tassie.

4 beurre bosc pears, cored and halved
200 g Pyengana or other top-quality cheddar
4 thick slices sourdough bread

SULTANA CHUTNEY
350 g sultanas
6 spring onions, white and pale-green parts only,
**   sliced diagonally**
1 cup (250 ml) cider vinegar
1¼ cups (275 g) brown sugar
1½–2 cm piece ginger, grated
2 cloves garlic, crushed or grated
1 teaspoon ground cinnamon
½ teaspoon allspice
½ cup slivered almonds
2 tablespoons water

1 To make the chutney, combine all ingredients in a saucepan over high heat, stirring well. Bring to the boil, then simmer over low heat for about 25 minutes, until the mixture thickens, stirring occasionally. Set aside.
2 Place the pears face-down on a preheated chargrill over high heat and cook for about 2–3 minutes on each side. Toast the bread at the same time, placing it face-down on the chargrill and cooking for about 1 minute on each side.
3 To serve, place a piece of toast, two pear halves and a couple of chunks of cheese on each plate, with a big dollop of the chutney on the side.

Serves 4

Peaches stuffed with amaretti biscuits and a strawberry coulis

PREP **15 mins** COOK **20 mins**

Australian summers are all about stone fruit. You can smell the peaches, mangoes and apricots the moment you walk into a fruit shop.

You could simply grill any of these fruits for a delicious result, but here is a quick baked dish, with the peaches stuffed with Italian amaretti biscuits for something different. One hint – make sure you use freestone peaches, because, as their name suggests, their stones can be easily removed, which makes it much easier.

5 freestone peaches, peeled, halved and
**   seeds discarded**
4 (80 g) amaretti biscuits
1 free-range or organic egg yolk
50 g caster sugar
50 g unsalted butter

STRAWBERRY COULIS
150 g strawberries
2 tablespoons caster sugar
1 teaspoon lemon juice
2 tablespoons water

1 First, eat half a delicious peach because you only need four and a half for the recipe.
2 Preheat the barbecue to very hot.
3 Place the amaretti biscuits in a food processor and blend to make coarse crumbs. Chop the remaining peach half into small pieces and add it, with the egg yolk and sugar, to the amaretti mix, and blend for a few seconds to combine.
4 Grease a small baking dish with half the butter and place eight peach halves, cut-side up, snugly in the dish. Spoon the amaretti mixture into the peach cavities, and top with a little of the remaining butter.
5 Place the baking dish in the middle of the barbecue with heat surrounding it on both sides, but not directly underneath. Close the hood and cook for about 20 minutes, or until the peaches are just tender and the filling is set.
6 While the peaches are baking, clean the bowl of the food processor and make the coulis. Place all the ingredients in the food processor and blend until smooth.
7 Remove the baking dish from the barbecue and place two stuffed peach halves on each plate with a little coulis drizzled over the top.

Serves 4

DESSERT

Black label rocky road

PREP **10 mins** COOK **2–6 mins** REST **2 hrs (in refrigerator)**

If you want to make yourself a very popular guest at a friend's dinner or if your kid beat up the neighbour's brat or your dog ate their cat – this will fix it. Guaranteed.

I cheat and make this in a rectangular takeaway container in the microwave. Just make sure that you use really, really good dark chocolate – one with 70 per cent cocoa solids.

2 tablespoons raisins
2 tablespoons brandy
400 g best-quality dark chocolate
8 marshmallows, halved
50 g shelled, unsalted pistachio nuts

1 Soak raisins in brandy in a small bowl for half an hour.
2 The cheat's way to melt the chocolate is to place it, broken into small pieces, in a takeaway food container and microwave on medium for 1–2 minutes, then stir the melted chocolate until it is smooth. Alternatively, you could melt the chocolate in a double boiler (if you have one) or over hot water. To do this, bring a saucepan of water to the boil, then turn the heat to very low. Place the chocolate in a large heatproof bowl that sits snugly on top of the saucepan (don't let the bowl touch the water) and allow to sit for 5 minutes. Make sure that no water or steam gets into the chocolate, or it will spoil. Stir the chocolate until it has completely melted.
3 Drain the raisins and discard brandy. If you have used a takeaway container, just stir the raisins, marshmallows and pistachios through the melted chocolate and refrigerate for about 2 hours until set. If you have used a double boiler or the hot water method, pour the chocolate into either a baking tray lined with baking paper, or a takeaway container, and stir through the raisins, marshmallows and pistachios and refrigerate for about 2 hours.
4 Remove from refrigerator and sit in hot water for a couple of seconds, then remove the rocky road from container and cut into pieces to serve, using a heavy kitchen knife, warmed under hot water if necessary.

Serves 8–10

Strawberry and marshmallow skewers with chocolate sauce >

PREP **10 mins** COOK **5–8 mins**

The downside of making this once is that the kids will want it every time you barbecue a snag.

Not a lot of genius involved, just a handful of supermarket ingredients. Again, make sure you use chocolate with 70 per cent cocoa solids.

Just beware of the potential stampede.

12 strawberries
8 marshmallows
150 g best-quality dark chocolate,
  broken into pieces
100 ml pouring cream

1 Thread the strawberries and marshmallows onto skewers and refrigerate until ready to use.
2 Heat cream in a small saucepan over high heat until it is just about to boil. Add the chocolate pieces and reduce the heat to a very low simmer, stirring for about 1 minute until the chocolate dissolves. Set aside.
3 Remove the skewers from the fridge and place them on a preheated lightly oiled chargrill over high heat. Cook for about 1 minute on each side, turning once, until the marshmallows begin to colour but before they melt.
4 Remove the skewers from the heat and place on plates. Drizzle the chocolate sauce over the top.

Serves 4 with demands for more

Five books in five years. Whew!

Firstly, my thanks to all of you who have bought the books. Penguin wouldn't keep inviting me back if the books weren't selling so well.

The Penguin team has been great to work with on each book and this one has been both the easiest and the most fun.

My thanks to Penguin head honcho, Julie Gibbs, for commissioning number five. To Art Director, Daniel New, and his design team, including Clio Kempster, for their creativity and effort – I love what they've done with the look of this. Also, to Nicole Abadee for translating my ramblings into English and editing me into some sort of sense. To Heidi McCourt for the PR on *The Great Aussie Asian Cookbook* that has given this one its momentum, and in advance for the great work I know she'll do on this.

But my special thanks go to Publishing Manager, Ingrid Ohlsson, my main contact at Penguin, who has seen me through the ups and downs of five books. She is an absolute professional and her patience, common sense and intelligence have made her a real pleasure to work with.

Photographer Rob Palmer has shot all five books and stylist Michelle (get your sausage fingers out of there Kimbo) Noerianto has worked on the past three. The three amigos had a ball with this book and really didn't want the shoot to finish. My thanks to them both and to Steve Brown for helping out when Rob was crook.

There have been some 700+ recipes in five years to write and test. I think I'll head out for dinner and eat someone else's food.

THANKS

INDEX

INDEX 203

VIKING

Published by the Penguin Group
Penguin Group (Australia)
250 Camberwell Road, Camberwell, Victoria 3124, Australia
(a division of Pearson Australia Group Pty Ltd)
Penguin Group (USA) Inc.
375 Hudson Street, New York, New York 10014, USA
Penguin Group (Canada)
90 Eglinton Avenue East, Suite 700, Toronto, Canada ON M4P 2Y3
(a division of Pearson Penguin Canada Inc.)
Penguin Books Ltd
80 Strand, London WC2R 0RL England
Penguin Ireland
25 St Stephen's Green, Dublin 2, Ireland
(a division of Penguin Books Ltd)
Penguin Books India Pvt Ltd
11 Community Centre, Panchsheel Park, New Delhi – 110 017, India
Penguin Group (NZ)
67 Apollo Drive, Rosedale, North Shore 0632, New Zealand
(a division of Pearson New Zealand Ltd)
Penguin Books (South Africa) (Pty) Ltd
24 Sturdee Avenue, Rosebank, Johannesburg 2196, South Africa

Penguin Books Ltd, Registered Offices: 80 Strand, London, WC2R 0RL, England

First published by Penguin Group (Australia), 2012

10 9 8 7 6 5 4 3 2 1

Design by Daniel New © Penguin Group (Australia)
Photography by Rob Palmer
Food styling by Michelle Noerianto
Typeset in ITC Franklin Gothic by Post Pre-press Group, Brisbane, Queensland
Colour reproduction by Splitting Image, Clayton Victoria
Printed and bound by Imago Productions, Singapore

National Library of Australia
Cataloguing-in-Publication data:

Terakes, Kim.
The great Aussie barbie fast & easy cookbook/by Kim Terakes; photographs by Rob Palmer.

9780670076192 (pbk.).

Barbecuing.
Other authors/contributors: Palmer, Rob.

641.5784

penguin.com.au